Oh Baby! Crochet™

Edited By Connie Ellison

HOUSE of
WHITE
BIRCHES

PUBLISHERS
SINCE 1947

Oh Baby! Crochet

Editor Connie Ellison

Art Director Brad Snow

Publishing Services Director Brenda Gallmeyer

Assistant Editor Judy Crow

Assistant Art Director Nick Pierce

Copy Supervisor Michelle Beck

Copy Editors Susanna Tobias, Judy Weatherford

Technical Editor Agnes Russell

Technical Artist Nicole Gage

Graphic Arts Supervisor Erin Augsburger

Book Design Nick Pierce

Graphic Artists Jessi Butler, Vicki Staggs

Production Assistant Judy Neuenschwanser

Photography Supervisor Tammy Christian

Photography Scott Campbell

Photography Assistant Martha Coquat

Oh Baby! Crochet is published by DRG, 306 East Parr Road, Berne, IN 46711. Copyright © 2010 DRG. All rights reserved. This publication may not be reproduced in part or in whole without written permission from the publisher.

First Printing: 2010, China
Library of Congress Number: 2008934502
Hardcover ISBN: 978-1-59217-256-6
Softcover ISBN: 978-1-59217-257-3

RETAIL STORES: If you would like to carry this pattern book or any other DRG publications, visit DRGwholesale.com

Every effort has been made to ensure that the instructions in this publication are complete and accurate. We cannot, however, take responsibility for human error, typographical mistakes or variations in individual work. Please visit AnniesCustomerCare.com to check for pattern updates.

1 2 3 4 5 6 7 8 9

DRGbooks.com

Welcome!

Everyone wants to make something special for a new baby, and a handmade gift is just about the nicest gift you can give to a family member or a friend. Whether you are crocheting for your own child, your grandchild or great-grandchild, or for a friend, you are sure to find projects in Oh Baby! Crochet that will express your love and, at the same time, create heirloom treasures for years to come.

And while you have your hooks out, it's a good time to remember those going through traumatic times with their little ones. During times such as these, it means a lot to the family just to know that someone thinks enough of their child to take the time out of their busy day for someone they may never know. Donations of hats, blankets and booties that are quick-to-stitch are much appreciated by your local children's hospital or women's shelter; these items are such a comfort for a baby born prematurely or with other health problems.

In Oh Baby! Crochet you'll find 65 beautiful designs ranging from quick-to-stitch to more intricate patterns.

The book is divided into four design-filled chapters. The Pretty Baby chapter includes a frilly dress for her, an heirloom-quality christening set for him, and matching his-and-her striped sweaters and hats. Baby Essentials has patterns for bibs and hats in all shapes and designs, a diaper cover and much more. Cuddle Baby is brimming with beautiful blanket and pillow sets and includes adorable papoose wraps. Baby Gifts is full of quick-to-stitch items including slippers, headbands, pacifier holders, edgings and the cutest little puppy and kitty you've ever seen!

We hope you have as much fun stitching these projects as we did putting this book together for you.

Happy stitching,

Connie

contents

pretty baby

Frilly Dress

Design by Diane Simpson

Skill Level

■■■□ INTERMEDIATE

Finished Sizes

Instructions given fit newborn–3 months; changes for sizes 3–6 months, 6–9 months and 9–12 months are in [ ].

Materials

- Red Heart Designer Sport light (light worsted) weight yarn (3 oz/279 yds/ 85g per ball):
  2 [2, 3, 3] balls #3570 iced violet
- Size I/9/5.5mm crochet hook or size needed to obtain gauge
- Yarn needle

Gauge

16 sc = 4 inches; 4 sc rows = 1 inch

Pattern Notes

Weave in loose ends as work progresses.

Join with slip stitch as indicated unless otherwise stated.

Chain-3 at beginning of round counts as first double crochet unless otherwise stated.

Special Stitches

Berry stitch (berry st): Insert hook in indicated st, yo, draw up lp, ch 3, yo, draw through both lps on hook.

Shell: 5 dc in indicated st.

V-stitch (V-st): (Dc, ch 1, dc) in indicated st.

Beginning V-stitch (beg V-st): Ch 4 (counts as first dc, ch 1), dc in same st as beg ch-4.

Large shell (lg shell): (4 dc, ch 1, 4 dc) in indicated st.

Large V-stitch (lg V-st): (Dc, ch 3, dc) in indicated st.

Baby Dress

Yoke Side

Make 2.

Row 1: Starting at empire waist, ch 20 [22, 24, 26], sc in 2nd ch from hook, sc in each rem ch across, turn. *(19 [21, 23, 25] sc)*

Row 2: Ch 1, sc in first st, [berry st *(see Special Stitches)* in next st, sc in next st] across, turn.

Row 3: Ch 1, sc in first 2 sts, [berry st in next st, sc in next st] across, ending with sc in each of last 2 sts, turn.

Rows 4–6 [4–8, 4–8, 4–10]: Rep rows 2 and 3 alternately.

First Strap

Row 7 [9, 9, 11]: Ch 1, sc in each of first 2 sts, berry st in next st, sc in next st, leaving rem sts unworked, turn. *(4 sts)*

Rows 8–13 [10–15, 10–17, 12–17]: Ch 1, sc in first 2 sts, berry st in next st, sc in last st. Fasten off.

2nd Strap

Row 7 [9, 9, 11]: Sk next 13 sts on row 6, **join** *(see Pattern Notes)* in next st, ch 1, sc in same st as beg ch-1, berry st in next st, sc in each of next 2 sts, turn. *(4 sts)*

Rows 8–13 [10–15, 10–17, 12–17]: Ch 1, sc in first st, berry st in next st, sc in each of last 2 sts, turn.

Sew shoulder seams.

Skirt

Rnd 1 (RS): Ch 3 [3, 4, 4] *(half of underarm ch)*, now working on opposite side of foundation ch on first Yoke, sl st in each ch across, ch 6 [6, 8, 8] *(underarm ch)*, now working on opposite side of foundation ch of 2nd Yoke, sl st in each ch across, ch 3 [3, 4, 4] *(2nd half of first underarm ch)*, join in first ch, **do not turn.** *(12 [12, 16, 16] chs, 38 [42, 46, 50] sl sts)*

Rnd 2 (RS): Ch 3 *(see Pattern Notes)*, V-st *(see Special Stitches)* in next ch, dc in next ch *(3 sts of first half of underarm ch)*, *working behind both lps of sl sts of rnd 1 *(work in opposite side of foundation ch of Yoke)*, [V-st in next ch, dc in next ch] across yoke*, [V-st in next ch, dc in next ch] 3 [3, 4, 4] times across underarm ch, rep from * to * once across opposite side of Yoke, V-st in next ch, dc in next ch, V-st in last ch *(3 sts of 2nd half of underarm ch)*, join in 3rd ch of beg ch-3, turn. *(25 [27, 31, 33] V-sts, 25 [27, 31, 33] dc)*

Rnd 3 (WS): Beg V-st *(see Special Stitches)* in same st as joining, [shell *(see Special Stitches)* in next V-st, V-st in next dc] around, join in 3rd ch of beg ch-4, turn. *(25 [27, 31, 33] shells, 25 [27, 31, 33] V-sts)*

Rnd 4 (RS): Ch 3, 2 dc in ch-1 sp of beg V-st, [V-st in 3rd dc of next shell, shell in ch-1 sp of next V-st] around, ending with 2 dc in same ch-1 sp as beg ch-3, join in 3rd ch of ch-3, turn.

Rnd 5 (WS): Ch 3, [shell in next V-st, V-st in next shell] around, ending with dc in same st as beg ch-3, ch 1, join in 3rd ch of beg ch-3, turn.

Rnds 6 & 7: Rep rnds 4 and 5.

Rnd 8: Rep rnd 4, **do not turn.**

Rnd 9: Ch 1, sc in each dc and each ch-1 sp around, join in first sc, do not turn. *(200 [216, 248, 264] sc)*

Newborn–3 Months Size Only

Rnd 10: Ch 3, dc in same st as beg ch-3, dc in each of next 3 sc, [2 dc in next sc, dc in next sc] twice, [2 dc in next sc, dc in each of next 3 sc] around, join in 3rd ch of beg ch-3. *(252 dc)*

3–6 Months Size Only

Rnd 10: Ch 3, dc in same st as beg ch-3, dc in each of next 3 sc, [2 dc in next sc, dc in each of next 3 sc] around, join in 3rd ch of beg ch-3. *[270 dc]*

6–9 Months Size Only

Rnd 10: Ch 3, dc in same st as beg ch-3, dc in each of next 3 sc, [2 dc in next sc, dc in next sc] twice, [2 dc in next sc, dc in each of next 3 sc] 4 times, [2 dc in next sc, dc in next sc] 3 times, [2 dc in next sc, dc in each of next 3 sc] around, join in 3rd ch of beg ch-3. *[315 dc]*

9–12 Months Size Only

Rnd 10: Ch 3, dc in same st as beg ch-3, dc in each of next 3 sc, [2 dc in next sc, dc in next sc] twice, [2 dc in next sc, dc in each of next 3 sc] 4 times, [2 dc in next sc, dc in each of next 3 sc] around, ending with 2 dc in last sc, join in 3rd ch of beg ch-3. *[333 dc]*

All Sizes

Rnd 11: Ch 1, sc in same st as beg ch-1, ch 1, sk next st, sc in next st, sk next 2 sts, 4 dc in next st, ch 1, 4 dc (**lg shell**—*see Special Stitches*) in next st, sk next 2 sts, [sc in next st, ch 1, sk next st, sc in next st, sk next 2 sts, 4 dc in next st, ch 1, 4 dc in next st, sk next 2 sts] around, join in first sc, sl st in next ch-1 sp, turn. *(28 [30, 35, 37] lg shells, 56 [60, 70, 74] sc, 56 [60, 70, 74] ch-1 sps)*

Rnd 12: Ch 5, sc in next ch-1 sp of lg shell, ch 2, [**lg V-st** *(see Special Stitches)* in next ch-1 sp, ch 2, sc in next ch-1 sp of lg shell, ch 2] around, ending with dc in same ch-1 sp as beg ch-5, ch 2, join in 3rd ch of beg ch-5, turn.

Rnd 13: Ch 3, 3 dc in same ch sp of lg V-st, sc in next ch-2 sp, ch 1, sk next sc, sc in next ch-2 sp, [lg shell in next ch sp of lg V-st, sc in next ch-2 sp, ch 1, sk next sc, sc in next ch-2 sp] around, ending with 4 dc in same lg V-st as beg ch-3, ch 1, join in 3rd ch of beg ch-3, turn.

Rnds 14 & 15 [14 & 15, 14–17, 14–17]: Rep rnds 12 and 13. At the end of last rnd, **do not turn.**

Rnd 16 [16, 18, 18]: Ch 1, sc in same dc as beg ch-1, *sc in next dc, hdc in each of next 2 dc, dc in next dc, dc in next sc, dc in next ch-1 sp, dc in next sc, dc in next dc, hdc in each of next 2 hdc, sc in next dc, sc in next ch-1 sp, rep from * around, join in beg sc, turn.

Rnd 17 [17, 19, 19]: Ch 5, sk next 2 sts, [V-st in next st, ch 2, sk next 2 sts] around, dc in same st as beg ch-5, ch 1, join in 3rd ch of beg ch-5, turn.

Rnd 18 [18, 20, 20]: Ch 3, 2 dc in same ch sp, shell in ch-1 sp of each V-st around, ending with 2 dc in same sp as beg ch-3, join in 3rd ch of beg ch-3, turn.

Newborn–3 Months Size Only

Rnd 19: [Ch 1, sl st in next st] around. Fasten off.

3–6 Months, 6–9 Months and 9–12 Months Sizes Only

Rnds [19 & 20, 21–24, 21–26]: [Rep rnds 17 and 18 alternately] [1, 2, 3] times.

Rnd [21, 25, 27]: [Ch 1, sl st in next st] around. Fasten off.

Neckline Trim

Rnd 1: Join yarn at shoulder seam, [ch 1, sl st in next st] around neckline opening. Fasten off.

Armhole Trim

Make 2.

Rnd 1: Join yarn at center underarm, [ch 1, sl st in next st] around armhole opening. Fasten off. ●

Hooded Baby Gown

Design by Joyce Nordstrom

Skill Level

■■■□ INTERMEDIATE

Finished Size

6–12 months

Finished Garment Measurement

Chest: 27 inches
Shoulder to bottom edge: 20 inches

Materials

- Red Heart Soft Baby light (light worsted) weight yarn (7 oz/575 yds/198g per skein): 1 skein each #7881 powder blue *(MC)*, #7321 powder yellow *(A)* and #7624 lime *(B)*
- Size G/6/4mm crochet hook or size needed to obtain gauge
- Yarn needle
- Sewing needle and thread
- 15mm blue buttons: 8

Gauge

20 sts = 4 inches; 22 rows = 24 inches

Pattern Notes

Weave in loose ends as work progresses.

Join with slip stitch as indicated unless otherwise stated.

Sleeper is worked in one piece from bottom upward to underarms, and then split for fronts and back.

Pattern

Row 1 (WS): Ch 1, sc in first sc, [ch 1, sk next st, sc in next st] across, turn.

Row 2 (RS): Ch 1, sc in each st across, turn.

Sleeper

Bottom Ribbing

Row 1: With MC, ch 23, sc in 2nd ch from hook, sc in each rem ch across, turn. *(22 sc)*

Row 2: Working in **back lps** *(see Stitch Guide),* ch 1, sc in each st across, turn.

Rep row 2 until piece measures 27 inches when slightly stretched. Fasten off.

Body

Working along end of rows, join A with sc in end of first row of Bottom Ribbing, [ch 1, sc in end of next row] across, making necessary adjustments to have 127 sts *(64 sc)* across row, turn.

Rep row 2 of Pattern.

[Rep rows 1 and 2 of Pattern alternately] twice. At the end of last rep, fasten off.

With B, [rep rows 1 and 2 of Pattern alternately] 3 times. At the end of last rep, fasten off.

Working as established in color pattern, work until piece measures 14½ inches, ending with a RS row.

Left Front

Maintaining color pattern and working Pattern rows, work across 33 sts, leaving rem sts unworked, turn. Continue working on 33 sts until Left Front measures 17½ inches total from beg, ending with a RS row, turn. Fasten off. Sk next 7 sts at neckline edge; reattach yarn in next st and work across rem 26 sts. **Dec 1 st** *(see Stitch Guide)* at neckline edge every row 7 times. Continue working in Pattern on 19 sts until piece measures 20 inches from beg. Fasten off.

Back

With WS facing, sk next 4 sts from Left Front, join yarn and work across next 67 sts, leaving rem sts unworked, turn.

Work in established color and Pattern until Back measures 20 inches as Left Front. Fasten off.

Right Front

With WS facing, sk next 4 sts from Back, work across rem 33 sts in Pattern. Continue working on 33 sts until Left Front measures 17½ inches total from beg, ending with a RS row, turn. Working in Pattern across 26 sts, leaving rem 7 sts at neckline edge unworked, turn. Dec 1 st at neckline edge every row 7 times. Continue working in Pattern on 19 sts until piece measures 20 inches from beg. Fasten off.

Sleeve Ribbing

Make 2.

Row 1: With MC, ch 9, sc in 2nd ch from hook, sc in each rem ch across, turn. *(8 sc)*

Row 2: Working in back lps, ch 1, sc in each st across, turn.

Rep row 2 until piece measures 7 inches when slightly stretched. Fasten off.

Sleeve

Working along end of rows, join A with sc in end of first row of Sleeve Ribbing, [ch 1, sc in end of next row] across, making necessary adjustments to have 37 sts *(19 sc)* across row, turn. Working in established color and Pattern rows, inc 1 st each side every 4th row 9 times. *(55 sts)*

Work even on 55 sts until piece including Sleeve Ribbing measures 7 inches. Fasten off.

Hood Ribbing

Row 1: With MC, ch 9, sc in 2nd ch from hook, sc in each rem ch across, turn. *(8 sc)*

Row 2: Working in back lps, ch 1, sc in each st across, turn.

Rep row 2 until piece measures 14 inches when slightly stretched. Fasten off.

Hood

Working along end of rows, join A with sc in end of first row of Hood Ribbing, [ch 1, sc in end of next row] across, making necessary adjustments to have 71 sts *(36 sc)* across row, turn. Work even on 71 sts until piece, including Hood Ribbing, measures 6 inches.

Hood Back

Working across 45 sts, leaving rem 26 sts unworked, turn. Working across next 19 sts, leaving rem 26 sts unworked, turn. Continue to work in Pattern on 19 sts until piece measures same length of unworked sts, approximately 5 inches. Fasten off.

Sew sides of Hood Back to edges of front portions.

Finishing
Right Front Band

Row 1: With RS facing, attach MC at lower Right Front, ch 1, sc in same st as beg ch-1, [ch 1, sk next st or next row end, sc in next st or next row end] rep up Right Front, ending at upper edge, turn.

Rows 2–6: Ch 1, sc in first sc, [sc in next ch-1 sp, ch 1, sk next sc] across, ending with sc in last sc, turn. At the end of last rep, fasten off.

Left Front Band

Row 1: With RS facing, attach MC at upper edge of Left Front, ch 1, sc in same st as beg ch-1, [ch 1, sk next st or next row end, sc in next st or next row end] rep down Left Front, turn.

Rows 2–6: Ch 1, sc in first sc, [sc in next ch-1 sp, ch 1, sk next sc] across, ending with sc in last sc, turn. At the end of last rep, fasten off.

Sew shoulder seams. Sew underarm seams of Sleeves; matching center Sleeve to shoulder, sew in place.

Matching edges of Hood to center tops of Front Bands, sew in place, easing in fullness as needed.

Sew buttons evenly sp on Right Front for boys and Left Front for girls. Use natural ch-1 sps for buttonholes on opposite edge.

Bottom Chain Weave

With 2 strands of MC held tog, make a ch approximately 30 inches long. Fasten off.

Weave through Bottom Ribbing over 2 rows, under 2 rows across edge. Pull ends to close opening, tie ends in a bow.

Chain may be removed and garment may be worn as a long cardigan for older children. •

Little Man Christening Set

Designs by Sue Childress

Skill Level

■■■□ INTERMEDIATE

Finished Size

Newborn–3 months

Materials

- Katia Cotton Comfort light (DK) weight yarn (1¾ oz/164 yds/50g per ball):
  4 balls #020 off white
- Size E/4/3.5mm crochet hook or size needed to obtain gauge
- Tapestry needle
- Sewing needle and thread
- 8mm white shank buttons: 8
- ¾-inch-wide non-roll elastic: 16 inches
- Stitch markers

Gauge

6 dc = 1 inch; 2 dc rows = ¾ inch

Pattern Notes

Weave in loose ends as work progresses.

Join with slip stitch as indicated unless otherwise stated.

Chain-2 at beginning of row or round counts as first half double crochet unless otherwise stated.

Chain-3 at beginning of row or round counts as first double crochet unless otherwise stated.

Special Stitches

V-stitch (V-st): (Dc, ch 1, dc) in indicated st.

Shell: (2 dc, ch 1, 2 dc) in indicated st.

Jacket
Bodice

Row 1: Beg at neckline, ch 77, hdc in 3rd ch from hook, hdc in each rem ch across, turn. *(76 hdc)*

Row 2: Ch 2 *(see Pattern Notes)*, hdc in each of next 13 hdc, **V-st** *(see Special Stitches)* in next hdc, hdc in each of next 8 hdc, V-st in next hdc, hdc in each of next 28 hdc, V-st in next hdc, hdc in each of next 8 hdc, V-st in next hdc, hdc in each of next 14 hdc, turn. *(72 hdc, 4 V-sts)*

Row 3: Ch 3 *(see Pattern Notes)*, dc in next 3 hdc, [sk next hdc, dc in next hdc, dc in sk hdc] 5 times *(front)*, **shell** *(see Special Stitches)* in next V-st, dc in each of next 8 hdc *(sleeve)*, shell in next V-st, dc in each of next 28 hdc *(back)*, shell in next V-st, dc in next 8 hdc *(sleeve)*, shell in next V-st, [sk next hdc, dc in next hdc, dc in sk hdc] 5 times, dc in each of next 4 hdc *(front)*, turn.

Row 7: Ch 3, dc in each of next 3 hdc, [sk next hdc, dc in next hdc, dc in sk hdc] 7 times, shell in ch-1 sp of next V-st, dc in each of next 16 hdc, shell in ch-1 sp of next V-st, dc in each of next 36 hdc, shell in ch-1 sp of next V-st, dc in each of next 16 hdc, shell in ch-1 sp of next V-st, [sk next hdc, dc in next hdc, dc in sk hdc] 7 times, dc in each of next 4 hdc, turn. *(28 4-dc groups, 6 dc)*

Row 8: Rep row 4. *(120 hdc, 4 V-sts)*

Row 9: Ch 3, dc in each of next 3 hdc, [sk next hdc, dc in next hdc, dc in sk hdc] 8 times, shell in ch-1 sp of next V-st, dc in each of next 20 hdc, shell in ch-1 sp of next V-st, dc in each of next 40 hdc, shell in ch-1 sp of next V-st, dc in each of next 20 hdc, shell in ch-1 sp of next V-st, [sk next hdc, dc in next hdc, dc in sk hdc] 8 times, dc in each of next 4 hdc, turn.

Row 10: Ch 2, working in **back lp** *(see Stitch Guide)*, hdc in each of next 21 dc, hdc in next ch-1 sp, ch 6 *(for underarm)*, sk sts of sleeve across to next ch-1 sp, hdc in each of next 44 dc across back, hdc in next ch-1 sp, ch 6 *(for underarm)*, sk sts of sleeve across to next ch-1 sp, hdc in next ch-1 sp, hdc across rem 22 dc, turn. *(92 hdc, 2 ch-6 sps)*

Row 11: Ch 2, working in back lps, hdc in each hdc and each ch across, turn. *(104 hdc)*

Rows 12–23: Ch 2, working in back lps, hdc in each st across, turn.

Row 24: Ch 3, dc in each of next 2 hdc, [sk next hdc, dc in next hdc, dc in sk hdc] 49 times, dc in each of next 3 hdc, turn. *(49 cross-sts, 6 dc)*

Row 25: Ch 3, dc in each of next 2 dc, [sk next dc, dc in next dc, dc in sk dc] 49 times, dc in each of next 3 dc, **do not turn.**

Edging

Rnd 1: Working on right front, ch 2, 2 hdc in end of each row to neck edge, 2 sc in first foundation ch, sc in each ch across neck edge, 2 sc in last ch, 2 hdc in each row down left front, 2 sc in first dc of bottom, sc in each dc

Row 4: Ch 2, hdc in each dc across, including the dc of each shell, V-st in each ch-1 sp of each shell, turn. *(88 hdc, 4 V-sts)*

Row 5: Ch 3, dc in each of next 3 hdc, [sk next hdc, dc in next hdc, dc in sk hdc] 6 times, shell in next ch-1 sp of V-st, dc in each of next 12 hdc, shell in next ch-1 sp of next V-st, dc in each of next 32 hdc, shell in next ch-1 sp of next V-st, dc in each of next 12 hdc, shell in next ch-1 sp of next V-st, [sk next hdc, dc in next hdc, dc in sk hdc] 6 times, dc in each of next 4 hdc, turn.

Row 6: Rep row 4. *(104 hdc, 4 V-sts)*

across bottom edge, 2 sc in last dc, **join** (see Pattern Notes) in beg sc.

Rnd 2: Ch 1, sc in each hdc along right front, 2 sc in last sc, [sc in each of next 4 sc, **sc dec** (see Stitch Guide) in next 2 sc] across neckline edge, 2 sc in last sc of neckline edge, sc in each of next 2 hdc, ch 2, sk next hdc (buttonhole), [sc in each of next 5 hdc, ch 2, sk next hdc] 7 times, sc in any rem sts, ending with 2 sc in last hdc, sc in each sc across bottom edge, join in beg sc.

Rnd 3: Ch 1, sc in each st around, working 2 sc in each ch-2 sp, working 2 sc in each outer edge corner, join in beg sc. Fasten off.

Row 4: Now working in rows, attach yarn to left neck edge, ch 1, [sc in each of next 2 sc, sc dec in next 2 sc] across neck edge, sl st in last sc of neck edge. Fasten off.

Sleeve
Make 2.

Rnd 1: Ch 2, work 33 hdc evenly sp around armhole opening, join in 2nd ch of beg ch-2. (34 hdc)

Rnd 2: Ch 2, working in back lps, hdc in each st around, join in 2nd ch of beg ch-2.

Rnd 3: Ch 2, work in **front lps** (see Stitch Guide), hdc in each st around, join in 2nd ch of beg ch-2.

Rnds 4–11: [Rep rnds 2 and 3 alternately] 4 times.

Rnd 12: Ch 3, dc in hdc before ch-3, [sk next hdc, dc in next hdc, dc in sk hdc] around, join in 3rd ch of beg ch-3. (17 cross-sts)

Rnd 13: Ch 3, dc in dc before ch-3, [sk next dc, dc in next dc, dc in sk dc] around, join in 3rd ch of beg ch-3.

Rnd 14: Ch 1, sc in each dc around, join in beg sc.

Rnds 15 & 16: Ch 1, sc in each sc around, join in beg sc. At the end of rnd 16, fasten off.

Sew buttons opposite buttonholes.

Booties
Make 2.

Sole
Rnd 1: Ch 10, hdc in 3rd ch from hook, hdc in each of next 6 chs, 5 dc in last ch, working on opposite side of foundation ch, hdc in each of next 6 chs, hdc in same ch as beg hdc, **join** (see Pattern Notes). (20 sts)

Rnd 2: Ch 2 (see Pattern Notes), hdc in same st as beg ch-2, 2 hdc in next st, hdc in each of next 7 sts, 3 dc in each of next 3 sts, hdc in each of next 7 sts, 2 hdc in next hdc, join in 2nd ch of beg ch-2. (29 sts)

Rnd 3: Ch 1, sc in same st, 2 sc in each of next 3 sts, sc in each of next 8 sts, 2 hdc in next st, 2 dc in each of next 5 sts, 2 hdc in next st, sc in each of next 8 sts, 2 sc in each of next 2 sts, join in beg sc. (41 sts)

Rnd 4: Ch 1, working in **back lps** *(see Stitch Guide)*, sc in each st around, join in beg sc. *(41 sts)*

Rnd 5: Ch 2, working in back lps, hdc in each st around, join in 2nd ch of beg ch-2.

Rnd 6: Ch 2, working in front lps, hdc in each st around, join in 2nd ch of beg ch-2.

Rnd 7: Ch 3 *(see Pattern Notes)*, dc in hdc before ch-3, [sk next hdc, dc in next hdc, dc in sk hdc] 20 times, sk next 2 hdc, [**dc dec** *(see Stitch Guide)* in next 3 hdc] twice, sk next 2 hdc, [sk next hdc, dc in next hdc, dc in sk hdc] 5 times, join. *(34 sts)*

Rnd 8: With stitch markers, mark off center front 12 sts, ch 3, dc in st before ch-3, [sk next st, dc in next st, dc in sk st] rep to center 12 sts, [dc dec in next 3 sts] 4 times, [sk next st, dc in next st, dc in sk st] around, join in beg ch-3.

Rnd 9: Ch 1, sc in each st around, join in beg sc. Fasten off.

Cap

Rnd 1: Ch 6, **join** *(see Pattern Notes)* to form a ring, ch 2, 13 hdc in ring, join in 2nd ch of ch-2. *(14 hdc)*

Rnd 2: Ch 2 *(see Pattern Notes)*, working in **back lps** *(see Stitch Guide)*, hdc in same st as beg ch-2, 2 hdc in each st around, join in beg ch-2. *(28 hdc)*

Rnd 3: Ch 1, working in **front lps** *(see Stitch Guide)*, [2 hdc in next st, hdc in next st] around, ending with 2 hdc in last st, join. *(42 hdc)*

Rnd 4: Ch 2, working in back lps, hdc in next st, [2 hdc in next st, hdc in each of next 2 sts] around, ending with 2 hdc in last st, join. *(56 hdc)*

Rnd 5: Ch 2, working in front lps, hdc in each hdc around, join.

Rnd 6: Ch 3 *(see Pattern Notes)*, working in back lps, dc in each of next 3 hdc, [2 dc in next hdc, dc in each of next 4 hdc] 10 times, dc in each of next 2 hdc, join. *(66 dc)*

Rnd 7: Ch 3, working in front lps, dc in each st around, join.

Rnd 8: Ch 3, working in back lps, dc in each st around, join.

Rnd 9: Rep rnd 7.

Rnds 10–13: Ch 3, dc in dc before ch-3, [sk next st, dc in next st, dc in sk st] around, join.

Rnd 14: Ch 1, sc in each st around, join.

Rnd 15: Ch 1, sc in each st around, join. Fasten off.

Pants

Rnd 1: Beg at waistline, ch 80, using care not to twist ch, **join** *(see Pattern Notes)* in first ch, ch 2, hdc in each ch around, join in 2nd ch of beg ch-2. *(80 hdc)*

Rnds 2–6: Ch 2 *(see Pattern Notes)*, hdc in each hdc around, join.

Rnd 7: Ch 3 *(see Pattern Notes)*, working in **front lps** *(see Stitch Guide)*, dc in each st around, join.

Rnd 8: Ch 3, working in **back lps** *(see Stitch Guide)*, dc in each st around, join, sl st in next dc.

Rnd 9: Ch 3, working in front lps, dc in each dc around, join, sl st in next dc.

Rnds 10–15: [Rep rows 8 and 9 alternately] 3 times.

First Leg

Rnd 16: Ch 3, dc in each of next 19 dc, sk next 40 dc, dc in each of next 20 dc, join. *(40 dc)*

Rnds 17 & 18: Ch 3, dc in dc before ch-3, [sk next dc, dc in next dc, dc in sk dc] around, join. *(20 cross-sts)*

Rnd 19: Ch 1, sc in each dc around, join. Fasten off.

2nd Leg

Rnd 16: Attach yarn in first free dc of rnd 15, ch 3, dc in each rem dc around, join. *(40 dc)*

Rnds 17–19: Rep rnds 17–19 of First Leg.

Finishing

Overlapping ends of elastic slightly, sew ends tog to form a circle. Encasing elastic ring, turn 6 rnds inward, folding opposite side of foundation ch to inside edge, touching rem lps of rnd 7, sew opposite side of foundation ch to rem free lps of rnd 7.

Sew crotch opening closed. •

Bonnet & Booties

Designs by Sue Childress

Skill Level
■■■□ INTERMEDIATE

Finished Size
Newborn–3 months

Materials
- Katia Cotton Comfort light (DK) weight yarn (1¾ oz/164 yds/50g per ball):
  5 balls #020 off white
- Size E/4/3.5mm crochet hook or size needed to obtain gauge
- Tapestry needle
- Sewing needle and thread
- 8mm pearl shank buttons: 8
- ¼-inch-wide off-white ribbon: 4 yds

Gauge
6 dc = 1 inch; 2 dc rows = ¾ inch

Pattern Notes
Weave in loose ends as work progresses.

Join with slip stitch as indicated unless otherwise stated.

Chain-3 at beginning of row counts as first double crochet unless otherwise stated.

Special Stitch
5-double crochet cluster (5-dc cl): [Yo, insert hook in indicated st, yo, draw up lp, yo, draw through 2 lps on hook] 5 times in same st, yo, draw through all 6 lps on hook, ch 1.

Bonnet
Rnd 1: Ch 6, **join** (see Pattern Notes) in first ch to form a ring, ch 3, 11 dc in ring, join in 3rd ch of beg ch-3. (12 dc)

Rnd 2: Ch 3, dc in same st as beg ch-3, 2 dc in each dc around, join in 3rd ch of beg ch-3. (24 dc)

Rnd 3: Ch 3, dc in same dc as beg ch-3, dc in next dc, [2 dc in next dc, dc in next dc] around, join in 3rd ch of beg ch-3. (36 dc)

Rnd 4: Sl st in next dc, ch 3, 2 dc in same dc, sk next dc, **5-dc cl** (see Special Stitches) in next dc, [sk next dc, 3 dc in next dc, sk next dc, 5-dc cl in next dc] around, join in 3rd ch of beg ch-3. (9 cls, 9 groups 3-dc)

Rnd 5: Sl st in next 2 dc, [ch 3, sc in next ch-1 sp of 5-dc cl, ch 3, sk next 2 dc, sc in next dc] around. (18 ch-3 sps)

Rnd 6: Sl st into ch-3 sp, ch 3, 4 dc in same ch-3 sp, 5 dc in each ch-3 sp around, join in 3rd ch of beg ch-3. (90 dc)

Rnds 7 & 8: Sl st in next 2 dc, ch 3, 4 dc in same dc, 5 dc in 3rd dc of each 5-dc group, sl st to join in 3rd ch of beg ch-3.

Row 9: Now working in rows, sl st in next 2 dc, ch 3, 4 dc in same dc, [5 dc in 3rd dc of next 5-dc group] 14 times, leaving rem 3 groups of 5-dc unworked, turn. (15 groups 5-dc)

Row 10: Sl st in 3rd dc, ch 3, 4 dc in same dc, [5-dc cl in 3rd dc of next 5-dc group, 5 dc in 3rd dc of next 5-dc group] across, turn. (7 cls, 8 groups 5-dc)

Row 11: [Ch 3 (see Pattern Notes), sk next dc, sc in next dc] twice, *ch 3, sk next 5-dc cl, [ch 3, sk next dc, sc in next dc] twice, rep from * across, turn. (23 ch-3 sps)

Row 12: Sl st into ch-3 sp, ch 3, 2 dc in same sp, 3 dc in each ch-3 sp across, turn. *(69 dc)*

Row 13: Sl st into 2nd dc, [ch 2, sk next 2 dc, 5-dc cl in next dc, ch 2, sk next 2 dc, sc in next dc] across, turn. *(11 cls)*

Row 14: Sl st in ch-2 sp, ch 1, sc in same ch-2 sp, [ch 3, sc in next ch-2 sp] across, turn. *(21 ch-3 sps)*

Row 15: Sl st into first ch-3 sp, ch 3, 4 dc in same sp, [ch 1, sc in next ch sp, ch 1, 5 dc in next ch sp] across, **do not turn.**

Row 16: Working across ends of row of Bonnet, work 2 sc in side edge of each row to rnd 8, sc in each rem st of rnd 8, work 2 sc in side edge of each row to end of row 15, ch 28 *(neck strap)*, dc in 5th ch from hook, dc in each rem ch across. Fasten off.

Sew button on opposite edge of Strap, use natural sp for buttonhole.

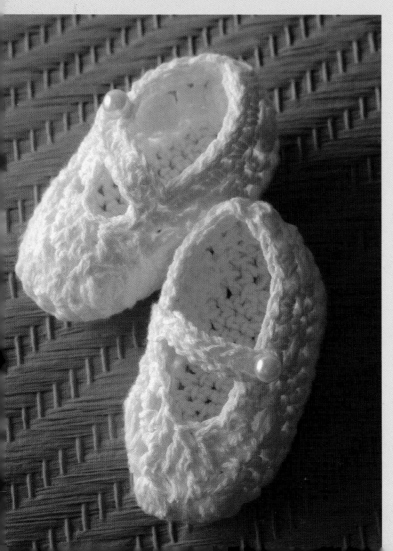

Booties
Make 2.

Sole
Rnd 1: Ch 12, 2 hdc in 3rd ch from hook, hdc in next ch, sc in each of next 6 chs, hdc in next ch, 5 dc in last ch, working on opposite side of foundation ch, hdc in next ch, sc in each of next 6 chs, hdc in next ch, 2 hdc in same ch as beg hdc sts, **join** *(see Pattern Notes)* in beg hdc. *(26 sts)*

Rnd 2: Ch 2, hdc in next ch, 2 hdc in next ch, sc in each of next 7 sts, hdc in next st, dc in next st, 2 dc in each of next 3 sts, dc in next st, hdc in next st, sc in each of next 7 sts, 2 hdc in next st, hdc in next st, hdc in same st as beg ch-2, join in 2nd ch of ch-2. *(32 sts)*

Rnd 3: Ch 2, hdc in each of next 12 sts, [2 dc in next st, dc in next st] 4 times, hdc in each of next 11 sts, join in 2nd ch of ch-2. *(36 sts)*

Rnd 4: Ch 3, **bpdc** *(see Stitch Guide)* in each st around, join in 3rd ch of ch-3. *(36 sts)*

Rnd 5: Ch 2, hdc in next st, **5-dc cl** *(see Special Stitches)* in next st, sk next st, [hdc in each of next 2 hdc, 5-dc cl in next st, sk next st] around, join in 2nd ch of ch-2. *(9 cls, 18 dc)*

Rnd 6: [Ch 2, sk next hdc, sc in next hdc, ch 2, sc in next ch-1 sp of cl] around. *(18 ch-2 sps)*

Rnd 7: Ch 2, hdc in same sp, 2 hdc in each of next 5 ch-2 sps, [**dc dec** *(see Stitch Guide)* in next 2 ch-2 sps] 3 times, 2 hdc in each of next 6 ch-2 sps, join.

Left Strap
Row 8: Sl st across next 9 sts, ch 10, hdc in 4th ch from hook, hdc in each rem ch across, sl st in next st of Bootie. Fasten off.

Right Strap
Row 8: Turn, sl st in next 9 sts, ch 10, hdc in 4th ch from hook, hdc in each rem ch across, sl st in next st of Bootie. Fasten off.

Sew button on Bootie opposite strap. Use natural sp at end of Strap for buttonhole. ●

Boy's Striped Hat & Sweater

Designs by Dianne Stein

Skill Level

■■■□ INTERMEDIATE

Finished Size
Newborn

Finished Garment Measurements
Sweater chest: 15 inches
Hat circumference: 11 inches

Materials
- Wendy/Peter Pan Supreme Luxury Cotton 4-ply (fine) sport weight yarn (292 yds/100g per ball): 2 balls each #1820 white *(A)*, #1818 sky blue *(B)*, #1859 green *(C)* and #1857 lilac *(D)*
- Size E/4/3.5mm crochet hook or size needed to obtain gauge
- Yarn needle
- 18mm dragonfly novelty button
- 15mm roller skate novelty buttons: 4
- Stitch markers

Gauge
9 dc = 1½ inches; 7 dc rows = 4 inches

Pattern Notes
Weave in loose ends as work progresses.

Join with slip stitch as indicated unless otherwise stated.

Chain-3 at beginning of row or round counts as first double crochet throughout unless otherwise stated.

Hat
Ribbing
Row 1: With B, ch 7, sc in 2nd ch from hook, sc in each rem ch across, turn. *(6 sc)*

Row 2: Ch 1, working in **back lps** *(see Stitch Guide)*, sc in each st across, turn

Rows 3–60: Rep row 2.

Row 61: Holding opposite side of foundation ch to row 60, working through both thicknesses, sl st in each of next 6 sts. **Do not fasten off.**

Body

Rnd 1 (WS): Working in side edge of Ribbing, ch 1, sc in side edge of row 1, work 1 sc in each of next 59 rows, **join** (see Pattern Notes) in beg sc. Fasten off. (60 sc)

Rnd 2: Working in back lps, join A in first st, **ch 3** (see Pattern Notes), dc in each st around, join in 3rd ch of beg ch-3, turn.

Rnd 3 (RS): Ch 3, dc in each dc around, join in 3rd ch of ch-3, **do not turn**.

Rnd 4: Ch 3, dc in each dc around, join in 3rd ch of beg ch 3. Fasten off.

Rnd 5: Join C in first st, ch 3, dc in same st as beg ch-3, sk next dc, [2 dc in next dc, sk next dc] around, join in 3rd ch of beg ch-3. Fasten off.

Rnds 6 & 7: Join A with sc in first dc, sc in each dc around, join in first sc. Fasten off.

Rnd 8: Join D in first sc, ch 3, dc in each sc around, join in 3rd ch of beg ch-3.

Rnd 9: Ch 1, sc in each dc around, join in beg sc. Fasten off.

Rnd 10: Join A with sc in first st, sc in each sc around, join in first sc. Fasten off.

Rnd 11: Join B with sc in first sc, sc in each st around, join in beg sc.

Rnd 12: Ch 4 (counts as first dc, ch 1), sk next sc, [dc in next sc, ch 1, sk next sc] around, join in 3rd ch of beg ch-4.

Rnd 13: Ch 1, sc in same dc as beg ch-1, sc in next ch-1 sp, [sc in next dc, sc in next ch-1 sp] around, join in beg sc. Fasten off. (60 sc)

Rnd 14: Join A in first sc, ch 1, sc in same sc as beg ch-1, sc in each sc around, join in beg sc. Fasten off.

Rnd 15: Join C in first sc, ch 3, dc in same st as beg ch-3, sk next sc, [2 dc in next sc, sk next sc] around, join in 3rd ch of ch-3.

Rnd 16: Ch 1, [sc in each of next 8 sc, **sc dec** (see Stitch Guide) in next 2 sc] 6 times, join in beg sc. Fasten off. (54 sc)

Rnd 17: Join A with sc in first sc, sc in each of next 6 sc, sc dec in next 2 sc, [sc in each of next 7 sc, sc dec in next 2 sc] 5 times, join in beg sc. Fasten off. (48 sc)

Rnd 18: Join D with sc in first st, sc in each of next 5 sts, sc dec in next 2 sc, [sc in each of next 6 sc, sc dec in next 2 sc] 5 times, join in beg sc. (42 sc)

Rnd 19: Ch 1, [sc in each of next 5 sc, sc dec in next 2 sc] 6 times, join in beg sc. Fasten off. (36 sc)

Rnd 20: Join B with sc in first sc, sc in each of next 3 sc, sc dec in next 2 sc, [sc in each of next 4 sc, sc dec in next 2 sc] 5 times, join in beg sc. (30 sc)

Rnd 21: Ch 1, [sc in each of next 3 sc, sc dec in next 2 sc] 6 times, join in beg sc. Fasten off. (24 sc)

Rnd 22: Join A with sc in first sc, sc in next sc, sc dec in next 2 sc, [sc in each of next 2 sc, sc dec in next 2 sc] 5 times, join in beg sc. Fasten off. (18 sc)

Rnd 23: Join B with sc in first sc, sc dec in next 2 sc, [sc in next sc, sc dec in next 2 sc] 5 times, join in beg sc. (12 sc)

Rnd 24: Ch 1, [sc dec in next 2 sc] 6 times, join in beg sc. (6 sc)

Rnd 25: Ch 1, [sc dec in next 2 sc] 3 times, join in beg sc. Fasten off. (3 sc)

Edging

Rnd 1 (WS): Working in opposite edge of Ribbing rows, join A with sc in side edge of row, sc in each of next 59 rows, join in beg sc. Fasten off. (60 sc)

Turn Ribbing rows and Edging upward onto Body of Hat.

Sew dragonfly button to center of rnd 26 of Hat.

Sweater
Body

Row 1 (RS): Beg at bottom edge of Sweater with B, ch 80, sc in 2nd ch from hook, sc in each rem ch across, turn. *(79 sc)*

Row 2: Ch 3 *(see Pattern Notes)*, dc in next sc, sk next sc, [2 dc in next sc, sk next sc] 37 times, dc in each of next 2 sc, turn.

Row 3: Ch 1, sc in each dc across. turn.

Rows 4–11: [Rep rows 2 and 3 alternately] 4 times.

Row 12: Rep row 2. Fasten off.

Row 13: Join A in first dc, ch 1, sc in same dc as beg ch-1, sc in each st across, turn.

Row 14: Ch 3, dc in next sc, [ch 1, sk next sc, dc in each of next 2 dc] 25 times, ch 1, sk next sc, dc in next sc, turn.

Row 15: Ch 1, sc in each st across, turn. Fasten off.

Row 16: Join D in first sc, ch 1, sc in same st as beg ch-1, sc in each sc across, turn.

Row 17: Ch 1, sc in first sc, [ch 1, sk next sc, sc in next sc] across, turn.

Rows 18–20: Ch 1, sc in first sc, [ch 1, sk next ch-1 sp, sc in next sc] across, turn. At the end of row 20, fasten off.

Row 21: Join A in first st, ch 1, sc in same st as beg ch-1, sc in each st across, turn. *(79 sc)*

Rows 22 & 23: Rep rows 14 and 15.

Row 24: Join C in first sc, ch 1, sc in same sc as beg ch-1, sc in each sc across, turn.

Right Front

Row 25 (RS): Ch 1, sc in each of next 18 sc, turn. *(18 sc)*

Row 26: Ch 1, sk first sc, sc in each of next 17 sc, turn.

Row 27: Ch 1, sc in each sc across, turn.

Row 28: Ch 1, sk first sc, sc in each of next 16 sc, turn.

Row 29: Ch 1, sk first sc at neckline edge, sc in each rem sc across, turn. *(15 sc)*

Row 30: Ch 1, sc in each sc across to last sc at neckline edge, leaving last sc unworked, turn. *(14 sc)*

Rows 31–34: [Rep rows 29 and 30 alternately] twice. *(10 sc)*

Row 35: Rep row 29. *(9 sc)*

Rows 36 & 37: Rep row 27.

Row 38: Ch 3, dc in each of next 8 sc, turn. *(9 dc)*

Row 39: Ch 1, sc in each dc across, turn.

Rows 40 & 41: Rep rows 38 and 39. Fasten off.

Left Front

Row 25: With RS facing, sk next 43 sts for Back, join C in 44th st, ch 1, sc in same st as beg ch-1, sc in each of next 17 sc, turn. *(18 sc)*

Row 26: Ch 1, sc in each sc across to last sc, leaving last sc unworked, turn. *(17 sc)*

Row 27: Ch 1, sc in each sc across, turn.

Row 28: Ch 1, sc in each sc across to last sc, leaving last sc unworked, turn. *(16 sc)*

Row 29: Ch 1, sc in each sc across to last sc at neckline edge, leaving last sc unworked, turn. *(15 sc)*

Row 30: Ch 1, sk first sc at neckline edge, sc in each rem sc across, turn. *(14 sc)*

Rows 31–34: [Rep rows 29 and 30 alternately] twice. *(10 sc)*

Row 35: Rep row 29. *(9 sc)*

Rows 36 & 37: Rep row 27.

Row 38: Ch 3, dc in each of next 8 sc, turn.

Row 39: Ch 1, sc in each dc across, turn.

Rows 40 & 41: Rep rows 38 and 39. Fasten off.

Back

Row 25: With RS facing, sk next 2 sc of row 24, join C with sc in next sc, sc in each of next 33 sc, leaving last 3 sc unworked, turn. *(34 sc)*

Rows 26–29: Ch 1, sc in each sc across, turn.

Row 30: Ch 3, dc in each sc across, turn.

Row 31: Ch 1, sc in each dc across, turn.

Rows 32–35: [Rep rows 30 and 31 alternately] twice.

First Shoulder Shaping

Row 36: Ch 3, dc in each of next 9 sc, turn. *(10 dc)*

Row 37: Ch 1, sk first st at neckline edge, sc in each of next 9 sc. Fasten off. *(9 sc)*

2nd Shoulder Shaping

Row 36: With RS facing, sk next 12 sts, join C in next st, ch 3, dc in each of next 9 sts, turn.

Row 37: Ch 1, sc in each of next 9 sc, leaving next st at neckline edge unworked. Fasten off. *(9 sc)*

Sleeve

Make 2.

Rnd 1: With C, ch 29, sc in 2nd ch from hook, sc in each rem ch across, join in beg sc. *(28 sc)*

Rnd 2: Ch 3, dc in each st around, join in 3rd ch of beg ch-3.

Rnd 3: Ch 3, dc in same st as beg ch-3, dc in each dc around to last dc, 2 dc in last dc, join in 3rd ch of beg ch-3. *(30 dc)*

Rnd 4: Rep rnd 2.

Rnd 5: Rep rnd 3. *(32 dc)*

Rnd 6: Rep rnd 2.

Rnd 7: Rep rnd 3. Fasten off. *(34 dc)*

Rnd 8: Join A with sc in first st, sc in each st around, join in beg sc.

Rnd 9: Ch 3, dc in same st as beg ch-3, [ch 1, sk next sc, dc in each of next 2 sc] 11 times, ch 1, join in 3rd ch of beg ch-3. *(24 dc, 12 ch-1 sps)*

Rnd 10: Ch 1, [sc in each of next 2 dc, sc in next ch-1 sp] 12 times, join in beg sc. Fasten off. *(36 sc)*

Rnd 11: Join D with sc in first sc, sc in each sc around, join in beg sc.

Rnd 12: Ch 1, sc in first sc, ch 1, sk next sc, [sc in next sc, ch 1, sk next sc] 17 times, join in beg sc. *(18 sc, 18 ch-1 sps)*

Rnds 13 & 14: Ch 1, sc in first sc, ch 1, sk next ch-1 sp, [sc in next sc, ch 1, sk next ch-1 sp] 17 times, join in beg sc.

Rnd 15: Ch 1, sc in first sc, sc in next ch-1 sp, sc in next sc, 2 sc in next ch-1 sp, [sc in next sc, sc in next ch-1 sp, sc in next sc, 2 sc in next ch-1 sp] 8 times, join in beg sc. Fasten off. *(45 sc)*

Rnd 16: Join A with sc in first sc, sc, sc in each sc around, join in beg sc. *(45 sc)*

Rnd 17: Ch 3, dc in next sc, ch 1, sk next sc, [dc in each of next 2 sc, ch 1, sk next sc] 14 times, join in 3rd ch of beg ch-3. *(30 dc, 15 ch-1 sps)*

Rnd 18: Ch 1, [sc in each of next 2 dc, sc in next ch-1 sp] 15 times. Fasten off.

Rnd 19: Join B with sc in first sc, sc in each sc around, join in beg sc. *(45 sc)*

Row 20: Now working in rows, sl st in each of next 4 sc, ch 1, sc in each of next 37 sc, leaving rem 4 sts unworked, turn.

Row 21: Ch 1, sk first sc, **sc dec** *(see Stitch Guide)* in next 2 sc, sc in each of next 31 sc, sc dec in next 2 sc, leaving last sc unworked, turn. *(33 sc)*

Row 22: Ch 1, sk first sc, sc dec in next 2 sc, sc in each of next 27 sc, sc dec in next 2 sc, leaving last sc unworked, turn. *(29 sc)*

Row 23: Ch 1, sk first sc, sc dec in next 2 sc, sc in each of next 23 sc, sc dec in next 2 sc, leaving last sc unworked, turn. *(25 sc)*

Row 24: Ch 1, sk first sc, sc dec in next 2 sc, sc in each of next 19 sc, sc dec in next 2 sc, leaving last sc unworked, turn. *(21 sc)*

Row 25: Ch 1, sk first sc, sc dec in next 2 sc, sc in each of next 15 sc, sc dec in next 2 sc, leaving last sc unworked, turn. *(17 sc)*

Row 26: Ch 1, sk first sc, sc dec in next 2 sc, sc in each of next 11 sc, sc dec in next

2 sc, leaving last sc unworked. Fasten off. *(13 sc)*

Sew front shoulders to Back shoulders, sew Sleeves into armhole opening.

Sleeve Trim
Make 2.
Rnd 1: Join A in opposite side of foundation ch of Sleeve, ch 1, sc in each ch around, join in beg sc. Fasten off. *(28 sc)*

Bottom Edging
Row 1: With RS facing and working in opposite side of foundation ch of Body, join B with sc in first ch, sc in each ch across, turn.

Row 2: Ch 3, dc in each sc across. Fasten off.

Sweater Trim
Row 1: With RS facing, join C in bottom edge of Right Front, ch 1, sc evenly sp up Right Front, around back neckline and down Left Front, turn.

Row 2: Ch 1, sc in each sc, turn.

Row 3: Ch 3, working in **back lps** *(see Stitch Guide)*, dc in each st up Right Front, around neckline and down Left Front, turn.

Row 4: Ch 1, working in **front lps** *(see Stitch Guide)*, sc in each st up Left Front around neckline and down Right Front. Fasten off.

Rnd 5 (RS): Now working in rnds, join A in Right Front bottom, ch 1, sc evenly sp up Right Front, around neckline and down Left Front, working 2 sc in bottom corner, sc in each dc across bottom edge, ending with sc in same st as beg sc, join in beg sc. Fasten off.

Sew buttons to Right Front of Sweater using natural sps between dc sts of row 3 of Sweater Trim for buttonholes. •

Girl's Striped Hat & Sweater

Designs by Dianne Stein

Skill Level

■■■□ INTERMEDIATE

Finished Size
Newborn

Finished Garment Measurements
Sweater chest: 15 inches
Hat circumference: 11 inches

Materials
- Wendy/Peter Pan Supreme Luxury Cotton 4-ply (fine) sport weight yarn (292 yds/100g per ball):
    2 balls each #1836 rose pink *(A)*, #1849 dusty pink *(B)*, #1857 lilac *(C)* and #1859 green *(D)*
- Size E/4/3.5mm crochet hook or size needed to obtain gauge
- Yarn needle
- 18mm pink rose novelty button
- 15mm buttons: 2 dark pink, 1 each sage and lavender
- Stitch markers

Gauge
9 dc = 1½ inches; 7 dc rows = 4 inches

Pattern Notes
Weave in loose ends as work progresses.

Join with slip stitch as indicated unless otherwise stated.

Chain-3 at beginning of row or round counts as first double crochet throughout unless otherwise stated.

Hat
Ribbing
Row 1: With C, ch 7, sc in 2nd ch from hook, sc in each rem ch across, turn. *(6 sc)*

Row 2: Ch 1, working in **back lp** *(see Stitch Guide)*, sc in each st across, turn

Rows 3–60: Rep row 2.

Row 61: Holding opposite side of foundation ch to row 60, working through both thicknesses, sl st in each of next 6 sts. Fasten off.

Body
Rnd 1 (WS): Working in side edge of Ribbing, join B with sc in row 1, work 1 sc in each of next 59 rows, **join** *(see Pattern Notes)* in beg sc. *(60 sc)*

Rnd 2: Ch 3 (see Pattern Notes), working in back lps, dc in each st around, join in 3rd ch of beg ch-3, turn.

Rnd 3 (RS): Ch 1, sc in each dc around, join in beg sc.

Rnd 4: Ch 3, dc in same st as beg ch-3, sk next st, [2 dc in next st, sk next st] around, join in 3rd ch of beg ch-3.

Rnd 5: Ch 1, sc in each dc around, join in beg sc.

Rnds 6 & 7: Rep rnds 4 and 5. At the end of rnd 7, fasten off.

Rnd 8: Join A with sc in first sc, sc in each sc around, join in beg sc.

Rnd 9: Rep rnd 4.

Rnd 10: Rep rnd 5. Fasten off.

Rnd 11: Join B with sc in first sc, sc in each st around, join in beg sc.

Rnd 12: Ch 3, dc in each sc around, join in 3rd ch of beg ch-3. Fasten off.

Rnd 13: Join D in first dc, sc in each dc around, join in beg sc.

Rnd 14: Ch 1, sc in each sc around, join in beg sc. Fasten off.

Rnd 15: Join B with sc in first sc, sc in each sc around, join in beg sc.

Rnd 16: Ch 3, 2 dc in same st as beg ch-3, sk next sc, dc in next sc, sk next sc, [3 dc in next sc, sk next sc, dc in next sc, sk next sc] 14 times, join in 3rd ch of beg ch-3. (15 groups 3-dc, 15 single dc)

Rnd 17: Ch 1, [sc in each of next 8 sc, **sc dec** (see Stitch Guide) in next 2 sc] 6 times, join in beg sc. Fasten off. (54 sc)

Rnd 18: Join C with sc in first sc, sc in each of next 6 sc, sc dec in next 2 sc, [sc in each of next 7 sc, sc dec in next 2 sc] 5 times, join in beg sc. (48 sc)

Rnd 19: Ch 1, [sc in each of next 6 sc, sc dec in next 2 sc] 6 times, join in beg sc. (42 sc)

Rnd 20: Ch 1, [sc in each of next 5 sc, sc dec in next 2 sc] 6 times, join in beg sc. Fasten off. (36 sc)

Rnd 21: Join B with sc in first sc, sc in each of next 3 sc, sc dec in next 2 sc, [sc in each of next 4 sc, sc dec in next 2 sc] 5 times, join in beg sc. (30 sc)

Rnd 22: Ch 1, [sc in each of next 3 sc, sc dec in next 2 sc] 6 times, join in beg sc. Fasten off. (24 sc)

Rnd 23: Join A with sc in first sc, sc in next sc, sc dec in next 2 sc, [sc in each of next 2 sc, sc dec in next 2 sc] 5 times, join in beg sc. (18 sc)

Rnd 24: Ch 1, [sc in next sc, sc dec in next 2 sc] 6 times, join in beg sc. (12 sc)

Rnd 25: Ch 1, [sc dec in next 2 sc] 6 times, join in beg sc. (6 sc)

Rnd 26: Ch 1, [sc dec in next 2 sc] 3 times, join in beg sc. Fasten off. (3 sc)

Edging

Rnd 1 (WS): Working in opposite edge of Ribbing rows, join A with sc in side edge of row, sc in each of next 59 rows, join in beg sc. (60 sc)

Rnd 2: Ch 1, 3 sc in same sc as beg ch-1, sk next sc, [3 sc in next sc, sk next sc] around, join in beg sc. Fasten off.

Turn Ribbing rows and Edging upward onto Body of Hat.

Flower

Rnd 1: With B, ch 7, join in first ch to form a ring, ch 1, [sc in ring, ch 3, 3 dc in ring, ch 3] 5 times, join in beg sc. Fasten off. (5 petals)

Sew Flower to center front of Ribbing with pink rose novelty button sewn in center.

Sweater
Body
Row 1 (WS): Beg at bottom edge of Sweater with A, ch 77, sc in 2nd ch from hook, sc in each rem ch across, turn. *(76 sc)*

Row 2: Ch 3 *(see Pattern Notes)*, dc in each sc across, turn.

Row 3: Ch 1, sc in each dc across. Fasten off.

Row 4: With WS facing and working in the opposite side of foundation ch of row 1, join B with sc in first ch, sc in each rem ch across, turn.

Row 5: Ch 3, dc in same st as beg ch-3, [sk next st, 2 dc in next st] 36 times, sk next st, dc in each of next 2 sts, turn.

Row 6: Ch 3, dc in same st as beg ch-3, [sk next dc, 2 dc in next dc] 37 times, turn.

Row 7: Rep row 6.

Row 8: Ch 1, sc in each st across, turn. Fasten off.

Row 9 (RS): Join C with sc in first st, sc in each st across, turn. *(76 sc)*

Row 10: Ch 3, dc in each of next 2 sts, ch 1, sk next st, [dc in each of next 4 sts, ch 1, sk next st] 14 times, dc in next 2 sts, turn. *(76 sts)*

Row 11: Ch 3, dc in each of next 4 sts, [ch 1, sk next st, dc in each of next 4 sts] 14 times, dc in next st, turn. *(76 sts)*

Row 12: Ch 1, sc in each st across. Fasten off.

Row 13 (WS): Join B with sc in first st, sc in each st across, turn.

Row 14: Ch 3, dc in same st as beg ch-3, dc in next st, [sk next st, dc in next st, sk next st, 3 dc in next st] 17 times, sk next st, dc in next st, sk next st, dc in each of next 2 sts, 2 dc in last st, turn. *(76 sts)*

Row 15: Rep row 12.

Row 16 (WS): Join D with sc in first st, sc in each st across, turn.

Row 17: Ch 3, dc in each sc across, turn.

Row 18: Rep row 12.

Row 19 (RS): Join B with sc in first st, sc in each st across, turn.

Row 20: Ch 3, dc in same st as beg ch-3, [sk next sc, 2 dc in next sc] 36 times, sk next st, dc in each of next 2 sts, turn. Fasten off.

Row 21 (RS): Join A with sc in first st, sc in each st across, turn. *(76 sc)*

Row 22: Ch 1, sc in each sc across, turn.

Right Front

Row 23 (RS): Ch 3, dc in each of next 2 sts, [ch 1, sk next st, dc in each of next 3 sts] 4 times, turn. *(19 sts)*

Row 24: Ch 1, sk first st, sc in each of next 18 sts, turn. Fasten off.

Row 25 (RS): Join B with sc in first st, sc in each of next 16 sts, turn. *(17 sc)*

Row 26: Ch 3, dc in each st across, turn. *(17 dc)*

Row 27: Ch 2, dc in each st across, turn. *(16 dc)*

Row 28: Ch 1, sk first st, sc in each of next 14 sts, turn. Fasten off.

Row 29: Join C with sc in first sc, sc in each sc across, turn. *(14 sc)*

Row 30: Ch 3, dc in same st, [sk next st, 2 dc in next st] 5 times, sk next st, dc in each of next 2 sts, turn.

Row 31: Ch 1, sk first st, sc in each of next 12 sts, turn. Fasten off.

Row 32: Join B with sc in first sc, sc in each of next 11 sc, turn.

Row 33: Ch 3, dc in next 2 dc, [ch 1, sk next st, dc in each of next 3 sts] twice, turn.

Row 34: Ch 1, sc in each st across. Fasten off.

Left Front

Row 23: With RS facing, sk next 38 sts for Back, **join** *(see Pattern Notes)* A in 39th st, ch 3, dc in each of next 2 sts, [ch 1, sk next st, dc in each of next 3 sts] 4 times, turn. *(19 sts)*

Row 24: Ch 1, sc in each of next 18 sts, leaving last st unworked, turn. Fasten off.

Row 25 (RS): Join B with sc in first st, sc in each of next 16 sts, turn. *(17 sc)*

Row 26: Ch 3, dc in each st across, turn. *(17 dc)*

Row 27: Ch 2, dc in each st across, turn. *(16 dc)*

Row 28: Ch 1, sc in each of next 14 sts, leaving last st unworked, turn. Fasten off.

Row 29: Join C with sc in first sc, sc in each sc across, turn. *(14 sc)*

Row 30: Ch 3, dc in same st, [sk next st, 2 dc in next st] 5 times, sk next st, dc in each of next 2 sts, turn.

Row 31: Ch 1, sc in each of next 12 sts, leaving last st unworked turn. Fasten off.

Row 32: Join B with sc in first sc, sc in each of next 11 sc, turn.

Row 33: Ch 3, dc in next 2 dc, [ch 1, sk next st, dc in each of next 3 sts] twice, turn.

Row 34: Ch 1, sc in each st across. Fasten off.

Back

Row 23: With RS facing, sk next 4 sts of row 22, join A in next unworked st, ch 3, dc in each of next 2 sts, [ch 1, sk next st, dc in each of next 3 sts] 6 times, ch 1, sk next st, dc in each of next 2 sts, turn, leaving rem 4 sts unworked. *(23 dc, 7 ch-1 sps)*

Row 24: Ch 1, sk first st, sc in each of next 28 sts, leaving last st unworked, turn. Fasten off. *(28 sc)*

Row 25 (RS): Join B with sc in first st, sc in each of next 27 sts, turn. *(28 sc)*

Row 26: Ch 3, dc in each st across, turn. *(28 dc)*

Row 27: Ch 3, dc in each st across, turn. *(28 dc)*

Row 28: Ch 1, sc in each of next 28 sts, turn. Fasten off. *(28 sts)*

Row 29: Join C with sc in first sc, sc in each sc across, turn. *(28 sc)*

Row 30: Ch 3, [sk next st, 2 dc in next st] 13 times, sk next st, dc in last st, turn.

Row 31: Ch 1, sc in each st across, turn. Fasten off.

Row 32: Join B with sc in first sc, sc in each of next 27 sc, turn.

Row 33: Ch 3, dc in next 2 dc, [ch 1, sk next st, dc in each of next 3 sts] 6 times, turn.

Row 34: Ch 1, sc in each st across. Fasten off.

Sleeve
Make 2.

Rnd 1: With C, ch 29, sc in 2nd ch from hook, sc in each rem ch across, join in beg sc. *(28 sc)*

Rnd 2: Ch 3, dc in each st around, join in 3rd ch of beg ch-3.

Rnd 3: Ch 3, dc in same st as beg ch-3, dc in each dc around to last dc, 2 dc in last dc, join in 3rd ch of beg ch-3. *(30 dc)*

Rnds 4 & 5: Rep rnd 2.

Rnd 6: Rep rnd 3. *(32 dc)*

Rnds 7 & 8: Rep rnd 2.

Rnd 9: Rep rnd 3. *(34 dc)*

Rnd 10: Rep rnd 2.

Rnd 11: Rep rnd 3. Fasten off. *(36 dc)*

Rnd 12: Join B in first dc, ch 3, dc in each dc around, join in 3rd ch of beg ch-3.

Rnd 13: Rep rnd 2.

Row 14: Now working in rows, sl st in each of next 4 sc, (sl st, ch 1, sc) in next sc, sc in each of next 27 sc, leaving rem 4 sc unworked, turn. *(28 sc)*

Row 15: Ch 1, **sc dec** *(see Stitch Guide)* in next 2 sc, [ch 1, sk 1 sc, sc in next sc] 13 times, turn. *(14 sc, 13 ch-1 sps)*

Row 16: Ch 1, sc dec in next 2 sc, [ch 1, sk next ch-1 sp, sc in next sc] 12 times, turn. *(13 sc, 12 ch-1 sps)*

Row 17: Ch 1, sc dec in next 2 sc, [ch 1, sk next ch-1 sp, sc in next sc] 11 times, turn. *(12 sc, 11 ch-1 sps)*

Row 18: Ch 1, sc dec in next 2 sc, [ch 1, sk next ch-1 sp, sc in next sc] 10 times, turn. *(11 sc, 10 ch-1 sps)*

Row 19: Ch 1, sc dec in next 2 sc, [ch 1, sk next ch-1 sp, sc in next sc] 9 times, turn. *(10 sc, 9 ch-1 sps)*

Row 20: Ch 1, sc dec in next 2 sc, [ch 1, sk next ch-1 sp, sc in next sc] 8 times, turn. *(9 sc, 8 ch-1 sps)*

Row 21: Ch 1, sc dec in next 2 sc, [ch 1, sk next ch-1 sp, sc in next sc] 7 times, turn. *(8 sc, 7 ch-1 sps)*

Row 22: Ch 1, sc dec in next 2 sc, [ch 1, sk next ch-1 sp, sc in next sc] 6 times, turn. *(7 sc, 6 ch-1 sps)*

Row 23: Ch 1, sc dec in next 2 sc, [ch 1, sk next ch-1 sp, sc in next sc] 5 times, turn. *(6 sc, 5 ch-1 sps)*

Row 24: Ch 1, sc dec in next 2 sc, [ch 1, sk next ch-1 sp, sc in next sc] 4 times, turn. *(5 sc, 4 ch-1 sps)*

Row 25: Ch 1, sc dec in next 2 sc, [ch 1, sk next ch-1 sp, sc in next sc] 3 times, turn. *(4 sc, 3 ch-1 sps)*

Row 26: Ch 1, sc dec in next 2 sc, ch 1, sk next ch-1 sp, sc dec in next 2 sc. Fasten off. *(2 sc, 1 ch-1 sp)*

Sew Sleeves into armhole openings.

Neckline Trim
Row 1: With WS of Neckline facing and working across Left Front, join D with sc in first sc, sc in each of next 10 sc, sc in next ch-1 sp of

Sleeve of row 26, sc in each of next 27 sc across Back, sc in next ch-1 sp of Sleeve of row 26, sc in each of next 11 sc of Right Front, turn. *(51 sc)*

Row 2: Ch 1, sc in each sc across, turn. Fasten off.

Row 3: Join C in first sc, ch 3, dc in each rem sc across. Fasten off. *(51 dc)*

Button Band
Row 1: Join C in side edge of row 26 of Left Front, ch 1, work 35 sc evenly sp to bottom edge, turn.

Row 2: Ch 1, sc in first sc, [ch 1, sk next sc, sc in next sc] 17 times, turn. *(18 sc, 17 ch-1 sps)*

Row 3: Ch 1, sc in first sc, [ch 1, sk next ch-1 sp, sc in next sc] 17 times, turn.

Row 4: Rep row 3. Fasten off.

Buttonhole Band
Row 1: Join C in bottom edge of Right Front, ch 1, work 35 sc evenly sp up Right Front through row 26, turn. *(35 sc)*

Row 2: Ch 1, sc in first sc, [ch 1, sk next sc, sc in next sc] 17 times, turn. *(18 sc, 17 ch-1 sps)*

Row 3: Ch 1, sc in first sc, *ch 3, sk next ch-1 sp, next sc and next ch-1 sp *(3 sts)*, sc in next sc, [ch 1, sk next ch-1 sp, sc in next sc] 3 times, rep from * twice, ch 3, sk next ch-1 sp, next sc and next ch-1 sp *(3 sts)*, sc in next sc, turn.

Row 4: Ch 1, sc in each sc and each ch across, **do not fasten off**, turn. *(35 sc)*

Outer Trim
Rnd 1: Ch 1, sc in each of next 35 sc up Right Front, sc evenly sp in side edge of rows to row 3 of Neckline Trim, sc in each dc across neckline, sc evenly sp down side edge of sts of Left Front to Button Band, sc in each st down Left Front, sc evenly sp across bottom edge of Sweater, turn.

Row 2: Now working in rows, ch 1, sc in first sc, sk next sc, 5 dc in next sc, sk next 2 sc, sc in next sc, [sk next sc, 5 dc in next sc, sk 2 sc, sc in next sc] across. Fasten off.

Neckline Scallop
Row 1: Join C with sc in 35th sc of Right Front Buttonhole Band, [sk next st, 5 dc in next st, sk next st, sc in next st] 4 times to neckline corner, [sk next 2 sts, 5 dc in next st, sk next 2 sts, sc in next st] 9 times across neckline, [sk next st, 5 dc in next st, sk next st, sc in next st] 4 times to Left Front Button Band. Fasten off.

Sleeve Trim
Make 2.
Rnd 1: Join A in opposite side of foundation ch of Sleeve, ch 1, sc in each of next 4 chs, [sc dec in next 2 chs, sc in each of next 4 chs] 4 times, join in beg sc. *(24 sc)*

Rnd 2: Ch 1, sc in same sc as beg ch-1, *sk next sc, 5 dc in next sc, sk next sc**, sc in next sc, rep from * around, ending last rep at **, join in beg sc. Fasten off. *(6 scallops, 6 sc)*

Sew buttons to Left Front opposite Buttonholes. ●

Baby Delight

Designs by Darla Sims

Skill Level

◼◼◼◻ INTERMEDIATE

Finished Sizes

Instructions given fit size 3–6 months; changes for size 9–12 months are in [ ].

Materials

- Medium (worsted) weight yarn:
    7 oz/350 yds/198g white
    3½ oz/175 yds/99g each lavender, mint and pink
- Size I/9/5.5mm [J/10/6mm] crochet hook or size needed to obtain gauge
- Tapestry needle
- Sewing needle
- White sewing thread
- ⅜-inch-wide pink satin ribbon: 1½ yds

Gauge

Size I hook: 3 sts = 1 inch; 7 dc rows = 4 inches; motif = 5 inches square
Size J hook: 5 sts = 2 inches; 3 dc rows = 2 inches; motif = 5½ inches square

Pattern Notes

Weave in loose ends as work progresses.

Join with slip stitch as indicated unless otherwise stated.

Chain-3 at beginning of row counts as first double crochet unless otherwise stated.

Special Stitch

Picot: Ch 3, sl st in 3rd ch from hook.

Sweater
Square Motif
Make 2.
Rnd 1: With size I [J] hook and pink, ch 4, 15 dc in 4th ch from hook, **join** (see Pattern Notes)

in top of ch-3. Fasten off. *(16 dc)*

Rnd 2: Join white with sc in any st, sk next st, 5 hdc in next st, sk next st, [sc in next st, sk next st, 5 hdc in next st, sk next st] around, join in first sc. Fasten off. *(4 sc, 4 groups 5-hdc)*

Rnd 3: Join mint with sc in 3rd hdc of any 5-hdc group, 7 dc in next sc, [sc in 3rd hdc of next 5-hdc group, 7 dc in next sc] around, join in first sc. Fasten off.

Rnd 4: Join lavender with sc in 4th dc of any 7-dc group, 9 tr in next sc, [sc in 4th dc of next 7-dc group, 9 tr in next sc] around, join in first sc. Fasten off.

Rnd 5: Join white with sc in any st, sc in each st around with 3 sc in 5th tr of each 9-tr group, join in first sc. Fasten off. *(48 sc)*

Matching sts, with white, sew one edge of Motifs together through **back lps** *(see Stitch Guide)*, forming strip.

Edging
Row 1: Working across short end of strip, join white with sc in first center corner st, sc in next 12 sts, turn.

Row 2: Ch 1, sc in each st across. Fasten off.

Rep rows 1 and 2 of Edging on opposite end of strip.

Back Body
Row 1: Working across long edge of strip, join white with sc in end of first row on Edging, sk next row, sc in st after center corner st of first Motif, sc in next 11 sts, sc in next seam, sc in next center corner st of next Motif, sc in next 11 sts, sk next end of row on Edging, sc in last row, turn. *(27 sc)*

Row 2: Ch 3 *(see Pattern Notes)*, dc in next st, 2 dc in next st, [dc in each of next 2 sts, 2 dc in next st] across, turn. *(36 dc)*

Rows 3 & 4: Ch 3, dc in each st across, turn. At end of last row, fasten off.

Right Front Motif

Rnds 1–3: Rep rnds 1–3 of Square Motif.

Row 4: Now working in rows, join lavender with sc in 4th dc of any 7-dc group, [9 tr in next sc, sc in 4th dc of next 7-dc group] 3 times, leaving rem sts unworked for front neck shaping. Fasten off.

Rnd 5: Now working in rnds, join white with sc in first st, sc in next 4 sts, [3 sc in next st, sc in next 9 sts] twice, 3 sc in next st, sc in last 5 sts, sc in 7 unworked sts of rnd 3, join in first sc. Fasten off. *(44 sc)*

Edging

Row 1: Join white with sc in first center corner st, sc in each of next 12 sts, leaving rem sts unworked, turn. *(13 sc)*

Row 2: Ch 1, sc in each st across. Fasten off.

Right Front Body

Row 1: Working across bottom of Right Front Motif, join white with sc in end of first row on Edging, sk next row, sc in next 13 sts, leaving rem sts unworked, turn. *(14 sc)*

Row 2: Ch 3, dc in next st, [2 dc in next st, dc in each of next 2 sts] 4 times, turn.

Rows 3 & 4: Ch 3, dc in each st across, turn. At end of last row, fasten off.

Left Front Motif

Work same as Right Front Motif.

Edging

Row 1: Join white with sc in 2nd center corner st, sc in each of next 12 sts, leaving rem sts unworked, turn.

Row 2: Ch 1, sc in each st across. Fasten off.

Left Front Body

Row 1: Working across bottom of Light Front Motif, join white with sc in end of first row on Edging, sk next row, sc in next 13 sts, leaving rem sts unworked, turn. *(14 sc)*

Rows 2–4: Rep rows 2–4 of Right Front Body.

Holding WS tog of Right and Left Fronts to Back with front neck shaping at top center; with white, matching sts and working in back lps, sew across each shoulder.

Front Opening Edging

Row 1: Working in sts and in ends of rows around front opening, join white with sc in row 4 of Right Front Body, sc in same row,

2 sc in each of next 2 rows, sc in next row, sc in each st around neck edge to row 1 of Left Front Body, sc in next row, 2 sc in each of last 3 rows. Fasten off.

Sleeve

Make 2.

Row 1: With white, ch 19, sc in 2nd ch from hook, sc in each ch across, turn. *(18 sc)*

Rows 2 & 3: Ch 3, dc in each st across, turn.

Row 4: Ch 3, dc in same st, dc in each st across to last st, 2 dc in last st, turn. *(20 dc)*

Row 5: Ch 3, dc in each st across, turn.

Rows 6–11: [Rep rows 4 and 5 alternately] 3 times. *(26 dc)*

At the end of last rep, fasten off. Matching center of last row on Sleeve to shoulder seam, sew Sleeve to armhole. Sew Sleeve side seam.

Bottom Ruffle

Row 1: Working across bottom of Body, join white in first st on left front, ch 3, (dc, ch 2, 2 dc) in same st; counting two joined sts at each seam as 1 st, *sk next 2 sts, (2 dc, ch 2, 2 dc) in next st, rep from * across rem sts of Left Front, Back and Right Front, turn. *(24 ch-2 sps)*

Row 2: Sl st in first 2 sts, (sl st, ch 3, 2 dc, ch 2, 3 dc) in next ch-2 sp, (3 dc, ch 2, 3 dc) in each rem ch-2 sp across, turn.

Row 3: Sl st in first 3 sts, (sl st, ch 3, 3 dc, **picot**—*see Special Stitch*, 4 dc) in next ch-2 sp, (4 dc, picot, 4 dc) in each rem ch-2 sp across. Fasten off.

For **first tie**, join white in st and end of row 1 on Left Front Body, ch 25, sl st in 2nd ch from hook, sl st in each ch across, sl st in same st on Body. Fasten off.

For **2nd tie**, join white in st 2 inches above last tie, ch 25, sl st in 2nd ch from hook, sl st in each ch across, sl st in same st on Body. Fasten off. Rep ties on opposite edge of Right Front Body.

Bonnet

Motif

Rnds 1–5: Rep rnds 1–5 of Sweater Square Motif. *(48 sc)*

Brim

Row 1: With WS of Square Motif facing, **join** *(see Pattern Notes)* white in any center corner sc, ch 3, dc in each of next 38 sc, leaving rem sc unworked, turn. *(39 dc)*

Rows 2–6: Ch 3, dc in each of next 38 dc, turn.

Row 7: Ch 3, (3 dc, **picot**—*see Special Stitch*, 3 dc) in next st, *sk next 3 sts, (3 dc, picot, 3 dc) in next st, rep from * across to last dc, dc in last st. Fasten off.

Fold first st of last row to end of row 5 and tack in place. Tack last st on opposite edge in same manner.

For **ties**, cut 2 pieces of ribbon, each 8 inches long. Tie each ribbon length into a bow. Cut 2 pieces of ribbon, each 18 inches long. Sew one end of each ribbon behind each bow. Sew 1 bow to each front corner. ●

baby essentials

Baby Biker Bibs

Designs by Paula Gron

Skill Level

■■■□ INTERMEDIATE

Finished Size

7¾ inches wide x 8¾ inches long

Materials

- Lion Brand Cotton-Ease medium (worsted) weight yarn (3½ oz/207 yds/100g per skein): 2 skeins #152 charcoal (MC)
- Lily Sugar 'n Cream medium (worsted) weight yarn (2½ oz/120 yds/71g per ball): 2 balls #01628 hot orange (CC)
- Size F/5/3.75mm crochet hook or size needed to obtain gauge
- Large-eyed tapestry needle

Gauge

13 sc = 3 inches; 7 sc rows = 1½ inches

Pattern Notes

Weave in loose ends as work progresses.

Join with slip stitch as indicated unless otherwise stated.

Each Bib requires one skein of each color.

Following the chart, bib is worked with nameplate first, from bottom to top. Carry the unworked color across wrong side, catching carried work every 6 or 7 stitches. Due to contrasting colors, do not work over carried yarn.

For Nameplate, follow Babe or Dude chart on page 46 as indicated.

Bibs

Center Nameplate

Row 1 (RS): With MC, ch 33, sc in 2nd ch from hook, sc in each rem ch across, turn. *(32 sts)*

Row 2 (WS): Ch 1, sc in first sc, **change color** *(see Stitch Guide)* to CC, drop MC to WS, sc in each of next 30 sc, catching MC periodically, change color to MC, drop CC to WS, sc in last sc, turn. *(32 sc)*

Rows 3–14: Ch 1, sc across, changing color as indicated by chart. At the end of row 14, fasten off.

Bib Bottom

Row 1 (RS): Working in opposite side of foundation ch, **join** *(see Pattern Notes)* MC in 2nd ch, ch 1, sc in same ch, change color to CC, drop MC to WS, sc in next sc, change color to MC, drop CC to WS, sc in each of next 26 chs, change color to CC, drop MC to WS, sc in next ch, change color to MC, drop CC to WS, sc in next ch, turn. *(30 sc)*

Rows 2 & 3: Ch 1, sc in first sc, change color to CC, drop MC to WS, sc in next sc, change color to MC, drop CC to WS, sc in each of next 26 sc, change color to CC, drop MC to WS, sc in next sc, change color to MC, drop CC to WS, sc in next sc, turn. *(30 sc)*

Rows 4–12: Follow chart rows 4–12, ch 1, sc in each st according to chart, changing color as indicated on chart, turn. *(2 sc)*

At the end of row 12, fasten off.

Bib Top

Row 1: Sk first st of row 14 of Center Nameplate, join MC with sc in 2nd sc, change color to CC, drop MC to WS, sc in next sc, change color to MC, drop CC to WS, sc in each of next 26 sc, change color to CC, drop MC to WS, sc in next sc, change color to MC, drop CC to WS, sc in next sc, turn. *(30 sc)*

Rows 2–11: Follow chart rows 2–11, ch 1, sc in each st according to chart, changing color as indicated on chart, turn. *(2 sc)*

At end of row 9, fasten off CC. At the end of row 11, **do not fasten off MC.**

Edging
Rnd 12: With RS facing, ch 1, sc in each st around outer edge, working 3 sc at each outer corner and sk 1 sc at each inside corner, join in first sc. Fasten off.

First Tie
Row 1: Join MC in side of Edging worked in row 11 of Bib Top at right edge, ch 51, sc in 2nd ch from hook, sc in each rem ch across. Fasten off.

2nd Tie
Row 1: Join MC in side of Edging worked in row 11 of Bib Top at left edge, ch 51, sc in 2nd ch from hook, sc in each rem ch across. Fasten off. ●

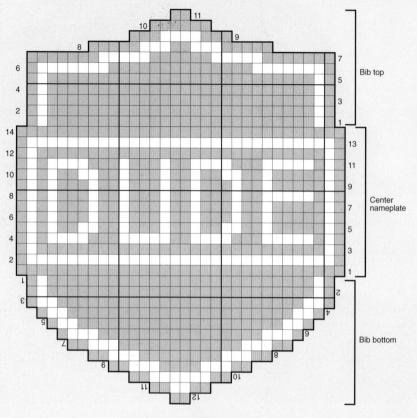

Boy's Biker Bib

COLOR KEY
- MC
- CC

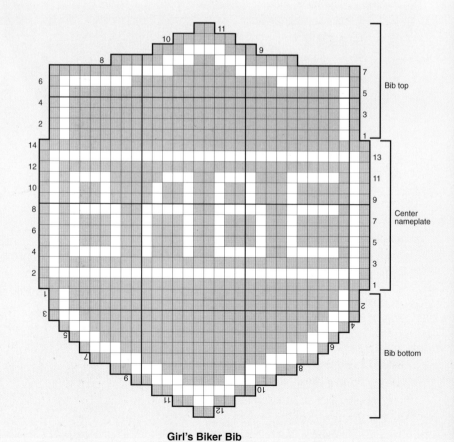

Girl's Biker Bib

Overall Bib

Design by Lucille LaFlamme

Skill Level

■■■□ INTERMEDIATE

Finished Sizes
Instructions given fit 6–12 months, changes for 12–18 months and 21–24 months are in [ ].

Materials
- TLC Baby light (light worsted) weight yarn (solids: 6 oz/490 yds/ 170g; sparkles: 5 oz/360 yds/141g per skein): 1 skein each #5322 powder yellow and #8322 powder yellow sparkle
- Size F/5/3.75mm crochet hook or size needed to obtain gauge
- Tapestry needle
- Sewing needle and thread
- 10mm white button

Gauge
5 dc rows = 1 inch

Pattern Notes
Weave in loose ends as work progresses.

Join with slip stitch as indicated unless otherwise stated.

Chain-3 at beginning of row counts as first double crochet unless otherwise stated.

Special Stitches
Shell: (2 dc, ch 1, 2 dc) in indicated st.

Picot: Ch 3, sl st in last sc.

Bib
Bodice
Row 1: With powder yellow sparkle, ch 6, sl st in first ch for button lp, ch 47 [50, 53], dc in 4th ch from hook, dc in each of next 4 [7, 10] chs,

shell *(see Special Stitches)* in next ch, dc in each of next 8 chs, shell in next ch, dc in each of next 12 chs, shell in next ch, dc in each of next 8 chs, shell in next ch, dc in each of next 6 [9, 12] chs, turn. *(40 [46, 52] dc, 4 shells)*

Row 2: Ch 3 *(see Pattern Notes)*, dc in each of next 7 [10, 13] dc, shell in next ch-1 sp, dc in each of next 12 dc, shell in next ch-1 sp, dc in each of next 16 dc, shell in next ch-1 sp, dc in each of next 12 dc, shell in next ch-1 sp, dc in each of next 8 [11, 14] dc, turn. *(56 [62, 68] dc, 4 shells)*

Row 3: Ch 3, dc in each of next 9 [12, 15] dc, shell in next ch-1 sp, dc in each of next 16 dc, shell in next ch-1 sp, dc in each of next 20 dc, shell in next ch-1 sp, dc in each of next 16 dc, shell in next ch-1 sp, dc in each of next 10 [13, 16] dc, turn. *(72 [78, 84] dc, 4 shells)*

Row 4: Ch 3, dc in each of next 11 [14, 17] dc, shell in next ch-1 sp, dc in each of next 20 dc, shell in next ch-1 sp, dc in each of next 24 dc, shell in next ch-1 sp, dc in each of next 20 dc, shell in next ch-1 sp, dc in each of next 12 [15, 18] dc, turn. *(88 [94, 100] dc, 4 shells)*

Row 5: Ch 3, dc in each of next 13 [16, 19] dc, shell in next ch-1 sp, dc in each of next 24 dc, shell in next ch-1 sp, dc in each of next 28 dc, shell in next ch-1 sp, dc in each of next 24 dc, shell in next ch-1 sp, dc in each of next 14 [17, 20] dc, turn. *(104 [110, 116] dc, 4 shells)*

Row 6: Ch 3, dc in each of next 15 [18, 21] dc, shell in next ch-1 sp, dc in each of next 28 dc, shell in next ch-1 sp, place stitch marker in the ch-1 sp of shell, dc in each of next 32 dc, shell in next ch-1 sp, dc in each of next 28 dc, shell in next ch-1 sp, dc in each of next 16 [19, 22] dc. Fasten off. *(120 [126, 132] dc, 4 shells)*

Body

Row 7: With RS of row 6 facing, **join** *(see Pattern Notes)* powder yellow in ch-1 sp of marked shell, remove stitch marker, ch 3, 2 [5, 8] dc in same ch-1 sp as beg ch-3, [dc in each of next 8 dc, 2 dc in next dc] 3 times, dc in each of next 9 [9, 9] dc, 3 [6, 9] dc in next ch-1 sp of shell, turn. *(45 [51, 57] dc)*

Row 8: Ch 3, dc in each of next 9 [12, 15] dc, *sk next 2 dc, shell in next dc, sk next 2 dc, [**fpdc** *(see Stitch Guide)* in next dc, dc in next dc] twice, fpdc in next dc, rep from * once, sk next 2 dc, shell in next dc, sk next 2 dc, dc in each of next 10 [13, 16] dc, turn. *(30 [36, 42] sts, 3 shells)*

Row 9: Ch 3, dc in each of next 9 [12, 15] dc, *sk next 2 dc, shell in next ch-1 sp, sk next 2 dc, [**bpdc** *(see Stitch Guide)* in next fpdc, dc in next dc] twice, bpdc in next fpdc, rep from * once, sk next 2 dc, shell in next ch-1 sp, sk next 2 dc, dc in each of next 10 [13, 16] dc, turn. *(30 [36, 42] sts, 3 shells)*

Row 10: Ch 3, dc in each of next 9 [12, 15] dc, *sk next 2 dc, shell in next ch-1 sp, sk next 2 dc, [fpdc in next bpdc, dc in next dc] twice, fpdc in next bpdc, rep from * once, sk next

2 dc, shell in next ch-1 sp, sk next 2 dc, dc in each of next 10 [13, 16] dc, turn. *(30 [36, 42] sts, 3 shells)*

Rows 11–22: [Rep rows 9 and 10 alternately] 6 times.

First Leg

Row 23 (WS): Ch 3, dc in each of next 4 [7, 10] dc, [bpdc in next dc, dc in next dc] twice, bpdc in next st, sk next 2 dc, shell in next ch-1 sp, [bpdc in next fpdc, dc in next dc] twice, bpdc in next fpdc, 2 dc in each of next 2 dc of next shell, dc in next ch-1 sp of shell, turn. *(20 [23, 26 dc, 1 shell)*

Row 24: Ch 3, dc in each of next 4 [4, 4] dc, [fpdc in next bpdc, dc in next dc] twice, fpdc in next bpdc, sk next 2 dc, shell in next ch-1 sp, sk next 2 dc, [fpdc in next bpdc, dc in next dc] twice, fpdc in next bpdc, dc in each of next 5 [8, 11] dc, turn.

Row 25: Ch 3, dc in each of next 4 [7, 10] dc, [bpdc in next fpdc, dc in next dc] twice, bpdc in next fpdc, sk next 2 dc, shell in next ch-1 sp, sk next 2 dc, [bpdc in next fpdc, dc in next dc] twice, bpdc in next fpdc, dc in each of next 5 [5, 5] dc, turn. *(20 [23, 26 dc, 1 shell)*

Rows 26–37: [Rep rows 24 and 25 alternately] 6 times.

Row 38: Ch 3, dc in each dc, dc in each post st, dc in ch-1 sp across. Fasten off. *(25 [28, 31] dc)*

2nd Leg

Row 23 (WS): Join powder yellow in center ch-1 sp of shell of row 22, ch 3, 2 dc in each of next 2 dc, [bpdc in next fpdc, dc in next dc] twice, bpdc in next fpdc, sk next 2 dc, shell in next ch-1 sp, sk next 2 dc, [bpdc in next dc, dc in next dc] twice, bpdc in next dc, dc in each of next 5 [5, 5] dc, turn. *(20 [23, 26 dc, 1 shell)*

Row 24: Ch 3, dc in each of next 4 [4, 4] dc, [fpdc in next bpdc, dc in next dc] twice, fpdc in next bpdc, sk next 2 dc, shell in next ch-1 sp, sk next 2 dc, [fpdc in next bpdc, dc in next dc] twice, fpdc in next bpdc, dc in each of next 5 [8, 11] dc, turn.

Row 25: Ch 3, dc in each of next 4 [7, 10] dc, [bpdc in next fpdc, dc in next dc] twice, bpdc in next fpdc, sk next 2 dc, shell in next ch-1 sp, sk next 2 dc, [bpdc in next fpdc, dc in next dc] twice, bpdc in next fpdc, dc in each of next 5 [5, 5] dc, turn. *(20 [23, 26] dc, 1 shell)*

Rows 26–37: [Rep rows 24 and 25 alternately] 6 times.

Row 38: Ch 3, dc in each dc, dc in each post st, dc in ch-1 sp across. **Do not fasten off.** *(25 [28, 31] dc)*

Edging
Row 1 (RS): Working up inseam, ch 1, 2 sc in side edge of each row, working down opposite inseam of Leg, work 2 sc in side edge of each row; working across row 38, **picot** *(see Special Stitches)* in first st, [sc in each of next 4 sts, picot] across, ending with picot in last st; working up outer side edge of Leg, [2 sc in side edge of each of next 2 rows, picot] rep across to Bodice; working on sts of Bodice row 6, [sc in each of next 4 sts, picot] rep across row 6, working in ends of rows up back opening, work 2 sc in side edge of each of next 6 rows. Fasten off. With RS facing, join powder yellow in side edge of row 1 of Bodice, ch 1, 2 sc in side edge of same row, 2 sc in side edge of each of next 5 rows, working on sts of Bodice row 6, picot in first st, [sc in each of next 4 sts, picot] rep across row 6, working down outer side edge of Leg, [2 sc in side edge of each of next 2 rows, picot] rep across to bottom corner, picot in corner st, [sc in each of next 4 sts, picot] across sts of row 38, join in beg sc. Fasten off.

Leg Strap
Make 2.
Row 1: With WS of Leg facing, join powder yellow in side edge of bottom of row 32 *(7th dc row from bottom upward)*, ch 22 [25, 28], sl st in side edge of last st at opposite edge of bottom of row 32, turn, ch 3, sl st in top of row 32, dc in each ch across, sl st in top of row 32 at opposite edge. Fasten off.

Finishing
Sew button opposite button lp at back neck. •

Duck Hooded Towel & Bath Mitt

Designs by Helen Heaverin

Finished Sizes
Towel: 28 x 28 inches
Small bath mitt: 5 x 6 inches
Large bath mitt: 6 x 8½ inches

Materials
- Lily Sugar 'n Cream medium (worsted) weight yarn (2½ oz/ 120 yds/ 71g per ball):
    7 balls #00010 yellow
    2 balls #01628 hot orange
    1 ball #00002 black
- Sizes E/4/3.5mm, H/8/5mm and I/9/5.5mm crochet hooks or sizes needed to obtain gauge
- Tapestry needle
- Stitch markers

Gauge
Size H hook: [sc, dc] 6 times and sc = 4 inches; 11 rows = 4 inches
Size I hook: [sc, dc] 3 times = 2 inches; 8 rows = 3 inches

Pattern Notes
Weave in loose ends as work progresses.

Join with slip stitch as indicated unless otherwise stated.

Chain-3 at beginning of row counts as first double crochet unless otherwise stated.

Duck Hooded Towel
Towel
Row 1 (RS): With size I hook and yellow, ch 84, dc in 2nd ch from hook, [sc in next ch, dc in next ch] across, turn. *(83 sts)*

Row 2: Ch 1, sk first dc, [dc in next sc, sc in next dc] across, ending with dc in ch-1, turn.

Rows 3–73: Rep row 2 until towel measures approximately 28 inches. Fasten off.

Hood
Row 1 (RS): Starting at bottom of Hood, with size I hook and yellow, ch 49, dc in 2nd ch from hook, [sc in next ch, dc in next ch] across, sc in last ch, place stitch marker at each end of row 1, turn. *(48 sts)*

Row 2: Ch 3 *(see Pattern Notes)*, sk next sc, **dc dec** *(see Stitch Guide)* in next dc and sc, [sc in next dc, dc in next sc] across to last 2 sts and end ch-1, dc dec in next sc and dc, sc in top of ch-3, turn. *(46 sts)*

Row 3: Ch 3, dc dec in next dc and sc, [sc in next dc, dc in next sc] across to last 2 sts and end ch, dc dec in next sc and dc, sc in top of ch-3, turn. *(44 sts)*

Rows 4–23: [Rep rows 3 and 4 alternately] 10 times. *(4 sts)*

Row 24: Ch 3, dc dec next 3 sts tog, sl st in top of ch-3. Fasten off.

Top Beak

Row 1: With size E hook and hot orange, ch 10, 2 sc in 2nd ch from hook, sc in each of next 3 chs, sk next ch, sc in each of next 3 chs, 2 sc in last ch, turn. *(10 sc)*

Row 2: Ch 1, sc in each sc across, turn.

Row 3: Ch 1, **sc dec** *(see Stitch Guide)* in next 2 sc, sc across to last 2 sc, sc dec in next 2 sc, turn. *(8 sc)*

Rows 4–7: [Rep rows 2 and 3 alternately] twice. At the end of last rep, fasten off. *(4 sc)*

Bottom Beak

Row 1: With size E hook, working in opposite side of foundation ch of Top beak, join hot orange with sc in first st, sc in same st, sc in each of next 3 chs, sk next ch, sc in each of next 3 chs, 2 sc in last ch, turn. *(10 sc)*

Rows 2–6: Rep rows 2–6 of Top beak. *(6 sc)*

Row 7: Rep row 3 of Top Beak. (4 sc)

Rnd 8: Now working in rnds, ch 1, sc evenly sp around outer edge of Bottom and Top Beaks, **join** *(see Pattern Notes)* in first sc, leaving 10-inch length of yarn. Fasten off.

Position Beak centered on Hood with foundation ch 3½ inches from edge, sew Bottom beak to Hood.

Eye

Make 2.

Rnd 1: With size E hook and black, make **slip ring** *(see illustration)*, work 6 sc in ring, tighten ring. *(6 sc)*

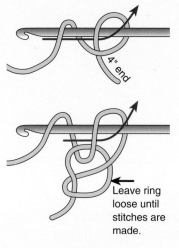

4" end

Leave ring loose until stitches are made.

Slip Ring

Rnd 2: 2 sc in each sc around. Leaving 6-inch length, fasten off. *(12 sc)*

Sew Eyes 1 inch above Beak with 1¾-inch sp between Eyes.

Hood Placement

With RS of Towel facing, measure 12 inches down from any corner and place stitch marker. Place another stitch marker 12 inches down on opposite side of same corner.

With RS facing, place Hood on top of Towel, matching stitch markers for placement of Hood.

Row 1: With size E hook, join yellow with sl st at stitch marker on right edge, working through both thicknesses, [ch 1, sl st] along side to within 2 sts from top corner, [ch 5, sl st in next st] twice, (sl st, ch 5, sl st) in top corner, working on opposite edge, [ch 5, sl st in next st] twice, [ch 1, sl st] in each st down side to next stitch marker. Fasten off.

Trim

Rnd 1 (RS): With size I hook, join hot orange with sl st in corner opposite Hood, working along edge of Towel, [sl st, ch 1] around and (sl st, ch 1) 3 times in corner, continue across front of Hood to other side of Towel and back down side edge of Towel, join with sl st in first st. Fasten off.

Bath Mitts
Large Mitt
Make 2.
Row 1: Beg at wrist, with size H hook and yellow, ch 18, dc in 2nd ch from hook, [sc in next ch, dc in next ch] across, turn. *(17 sts)*

Row 2: Ch 1, sk first dc, [dc in next sc, sc in next dc] across, ending with dc in ch-1, turn.

Rows 3–16: Rep row 2.

Row 17: Ch 1, sk first dc, **dc dec 3 sts tog** *(see Stitch Guide)*, [sc in next dc, dc in next sc] across to last 3 sts, dc dec 3 tog in last 2 sts and ch-1 sp, turn. *(13 sts)*

Rows 18 & 19: Rep row 17. At the end of row 19, fasten off. *(5 sts)*

Large Top Beak
Rows 1–7: Rep rows 1–7 of Towel Top Beak. *(4 sc)*

Large Bottom Beak
Rows 1–7: Rep rows 1–7 of Towel Bottom Beak.

Rnd 8: Rep rnd 8 of Towel Bottom Beak.

Sew Large Bottom Beak to center of front of Large Mitt.

Large Eye
Make 2.
Rnd 1: With size E hook and black, make **slip ring** *(see illustration)*, work 6 sc in ring, tighten ring. *(6 sc)*

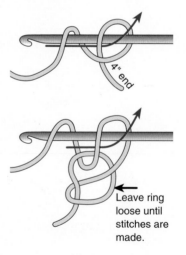

Leave ring loose until stitches are made.

Slip Ring

Rnd 2: 2 sc in each sc around. Leaving 6-inch length, fasten off. *(12 sc)*

Sew Eyes ½ inch above Beak with ¾-inch sp between Eyes.

Small Mitt

Make 2.

Row 1: Beg at wrist, with size H hook and yellow, ch 14, dc in 2nd ch from hook, [sc in next ch, dc in next ch] across, turn. *(13 sts)*

Row 2: Ch 1, sk first dc, [dc in next sc, sc in next dc] across, ending with dc in ch-1, turn.

Rows 3–11: Rep row 2.

Row 12: Ch 1, sk first dc, dc dec 3 sts tog, [sc in next dc, dc in next sc] across to last 3 sts, dc dec 3 tog in last 2 sts and ch-1 sp, turn. *(9 sts)*

Row 13: Rep row 12. Fasten off. *(5 sts)*

Small Top Beak

Row 1: With size E hook and hot orange, ch 6, 2 sc in 2nd ch from hook, sc in next ch, sk next ch, sc in next ch, 2 sc in last ch, turn. *(6 sc)*

Row 2: Ch 1, sc in each sc across, turn.

Row 3: Ch 1, **sc dec** *(see Stitch Guide)* in next 2 sc, sc in next sc, sc dec in next 2 sc, turn. *(4 sc)*

Row 4: Rep row 2.

Row 5: Ch 1, [sc dec in next sc] twice. Fasten off. *(2 sc)*

Small Bottom Beak

Row 1: With size E hook, working in opposite side of foundation ch of Top beak, join hot orange with sc in first st, sc in same st, sc in next ch, sk next ch, sc in next ch, 2 sc in last ch, turn. *(6 sc)*

Rows 2–4: Rep rows 2–4 of Small Top Beak. *(4 sc)*

Row 5: Ch 1, [sc dec in next 2 sc] twice, turn. *(2 sc)*

Rnd 6: Now working in rnds, ch 1, sc evenly sp around outer edge of Small Bottom and Small Top Beaks, join in first sc. Leaving 8-inch length of yarn, fasten off.

Sew Small Bottom beak to center of front of Small Mitt.

Eye

Make 2.

Rnd 1: With size E hook and black, make slip ring, work 6 sc in ring, tighten ring. Leaving 6-inch length of yarn, fasten off. *(6 sc)*

Joining

Row 1: Holding front and back of Mitt tog with front facing, with size H hook, join yellow with sl st in side edge of row 1 at right edge, [ch 1, sl st in next st] around to opposite side edge of row 1, ch 12, sl st in same st *(hanging lp)*, leaving opposite side of foundation ch open for Cuff. Fasten off.

Large Mitt Cuff

Make 2.

Row 1: With size E hook, join hot orange with sl st at bottom side seam, ch 7, sc in 2nd ch from hook, sc in each of next 5 chs, sl st in next 2 sts on Mitt, turn. *(6 sc)*

Row 2: Working in **back lps** *(see Stitch Guide)*, sk sl sts, sc in each of next 6 sts, turn.

Row 3: Ch 1, working in back lps, sc in each of next 6 sts, sl st in next 2 sts on Mitt, turn.

Rep rows 2 and 3 around wrist edge of Mitt. At the end of last rep, leaving 8-inch length of yarn, fasten off. Sew opposite side of foundation ch to last row.

Small Mitt Cuff

Make 2.

Row 1: With size E hook, join hot orange with sl st at bottom side seam, ch 5, sc in 2nd ch from hook, sc in each of next 3 chs, sl st in next 2 sts on Mitt, turn. *(4 sc)*

Row 2: Working in **back lps** *(see Stitch Guide)*, sk sl sts, sc in each of next 4 sts, turn.

Row 3: Ch 1, working in back lps, sc in each of next 4 sts, sl st in next 2 sts on Mitt, turn.

Rep rows 2 and 3 around wrist edge of Mitt. At the end of last rep, leaving 8-inch length of yarn, fasten off. Sew opposite side of foundation ch to last row. ●

Bon Appétit Bib

Design by Lindsey Stephens

Skill Level

■■□□ EASY

Finished Size

8½ inches wide x 13¾ inches long

Materials

- Coats Creme de la Creme medium (worsted) weight yarn (2½ oz/126 yds/71g per ball):
  2 balls #252 brite orange
- Size H/8/5mm crochet hook or size needed to obtain gauge
- Tapestry needle
- 1½-inch green button
- Stitch markers
- Straight pins

Gauge

8 sc = 2 inches; 9 sc rows = 2 inches

Pattern Notes

Weave in loose ends as work progresses.

Join with slip stitch as indicated unless otherwise stated.

Bib

Row 1 (RS): Ch 31, sc in 2nd ch from hook, sc in each rem ch across, turn. *(30 sc)*

Row 2: Ch 1, sc in each sc across, turn.

Rows 3–48: Rep row 2.

Row 49: Ch 1, sc in each of next 7 sc, place stitch marker *(7 sts for Button Strap to be worked later)*, sc in each of next 23 sc, turn.

Row 50: Ch 1, sc in each of next 7 sc, leaving rem 16 sc unworked for neck opening, turn. *(7 sc)*

Rows 51–64: Rep row 2. *(7 sc)*

Row 65: Ch 24, sc in 2nd ch from hook, sc in each of next 22 chs, sc in next 7 sc, turn. *(30 sc)*

Rows 66 & 67: Rep row 2.

Row 68: Ch 1, sc in each of next 23 sc, leaving rem 7 sc unworked, turn. *(23 sc)*

Row 69: Rep row 2.

Row 70: Ch 1, sc in each of next 23 sc, ch 6, sk next 6 sts of unworked sts of row 67, dc in 7th sc of row 67 *(buttonhole completed)*, turn. *(23 sc, 6 chs, 1 dc)*

Row 71: Ch 1, sc in dc, sc in each of next 6 chs, sc in each of next 23 sc, turn. *(30 sc)*

Rows 72 & 73: Rep row 2. At the end of last rep, fasten off. *(30 sc)*

Button Strap

Row 50: With WS facing, **join** *(see Pattern Notes)* yarn in marked 7th sc, ch 1, sc in same sc as beg ch-1, sc in each of next 6 sc, turn. *(7 sc)*

Rows 51–73: Ch 1, sc in each of next 7 sc, turn. At the end of row 73, fasten off.

Edging

With RS facing, fold bottom of Bib up so that row 1 rests on top of row 30. Use straight pins to keep folded section in place.

Rnd 1: Join yarn on side edge of Bib, ch 1, sc in same st as beg ch-1, sc evenly along edges of Bib, working through both thicknesses, sc along fold line and each side of pocket, around straps at top of Bib and working 3 sc in each outer corner around, join in beg sc. Fasten off.

Finishing

Cut 9-inch length of yarn, sew button to center RS between rows 69 and 70. •

Short Top Socks

Designs by Diane Simpson

Skill Level

■■□□ EASY

Finished Sizes

Instructions given fit newborn–3 months; changes for 3–6 months, 6–9 months and 9–12 months are in [ ].

Materials

- Red Heart LusterSheen fine (sport) weight yarn (4 oz/335 yds/113g per skein):
  Solid Socks:
  1 [1¼, 1½, 1¾] oz #0001 white or #0615 tea leaf
  Two-Color Socks:
  ½ [¾, ¾, 1] oz each #0001 white and #0615 tea leaf
- Size F/5/3.75mm, [G/6/4mm, H/8/5mm or I/9/5.5mm] crochet hook or size needed to obtain gauge
- Tapestry needle
- Stitch marker

Gauge

Size F hook: Rnds 1–3 = 1 inch; [**Size G hook:** Rnds 1–3 = 1¼ inches; **Size H hook:** Rnds 1–3 = 1½ inches; **Size I hook:** Rnds 1–3 = 1¾ inches]

Pattern Notes

Weave in loose ends as work progresses.

Do not join rounds unless otherwise stated. Use stitch marker to mark rounds.

Work all rows in **back loops** (see Stitch Guide) of each stitch unless otherwise stated.

Join rounds with slip stitch unless otherwise stated.

Short Top Socks
Solid Sock
Make 2.

Toe

Rnd 1 (RS): With size F [G, H, I] hook, make **slip ring** (see illustration), ch 1, 6 sc in ring, tighten ring, **do not join** (see Pattern Notes). (6 sc)

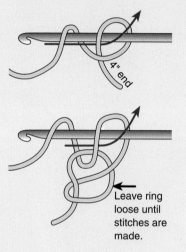

Leave ring loose until stitches are made.

Slip Ring

Rnd 2: 2 sc in each st around. (12 sc)

Rnd 3: [2 sc in next st, sc in next st] around. (18 sc)

Top

Row 4: Now working in rows, ch 18, sc in 2nd ch from hook, sc in each ch across, sl st in each of next 2 sts on Toe, turn. (17 sc)

Row 5: Sk sl sts, sc in each sc across, turn.

Row 6: Ch 1, sc in each sc across, sl st in each of next 2 sts on Toe, turn.

Rows 7 & 8: Rep rows 5 and 6.

Row 9: Sk sl sts, sc in each of first 8 sts, leaving rem sts unworked, turn. *(8 sc)*

Row 10: Rep row 6.

Rows 11–14: [Rep rows 5 and 6 alternately] twice, turn.

Row 15: Rep row 5.

Row 16: Ch 10, sc in 2nd ch from hook, sc in each rem ch across, sl st in each of next 2 sts on Toe, turn.

Rows 17–20: [Rep rows 5 and 6 alternately] twice, turn.

Row 21: Sk sl sts, sc in each sc across, turn.

Row 22: Turn WS out, working through both thicknesses, sl st rows 4 and 21 tog. Fasten off.

Flatten Sock, creating an L-shape, sew ends of rows tog to form heel.

Cuff

Rnd 1: Join *(see Pattern Notes)* in first st to left of heel seam, ch 1, sc in each st across row 8, sc in end of each of next 7 rows, sc in ch on opposite side of row 16, join in beg sc. *(25 sc)*

Row 2: Now working in rows, ch 7, sc in 2nd ch from hook, sc in next 5 chs, sl st in each of next 2 sts on rnd 1, turn.

Row 3: Sk sl sts, sc in each sc across, turn.

Row 4: Ch 1, sc in each sc across, sl st in each of next 2 sts on rnd 1, turn.

Rows 5–24: [Rep rows 3 and 4 alternately] 10 times.

Row 25: Turn WS out, working through both thicknesses, sl st row 24 and foundation ch on opposite side of ch-7 on row 2 tog. Fasten off.

Two-Color Sock
Make 2.

Toe

Rnds 1–3: With first color, rep rnds 1–3 of Solid Sock Toe. Fasten off. *(18 sc)*

Top

Row 4: Now working in rows, join 2nd color in first sc, ch 18, sc in 2nd ch from hook, sc in each ch across, sl st in each of next 2 sts on Toe, turn. *(17 sc)*

Rows 5–22: Rep rows 5–22 of Solid Sock Top.

Cuff

Rnd 1: With first color, rep rnd 1 of Solid Sock Cuff.

Rows 2–25: Rep rows 2–25 of Solid Sock Cuff. •

Fisherman's Hat

Design by Ellen Gormley

Skill Level

■■□□ EASY

Finished Size

Circumference: 16½ inches

Materials

- Bernat Handicrafter Cotton medium (worsted) weight yarn (1¾ oz/80 yds/50g per ball):
    2 balls #00085 jute
    1 ball #00083 cornflower
- Size G/6/4mm crochet hook or size needed to obtain gauge
- Tapestry needle
- Stitch marker

Gauge

7 sc = 1½ inches; 2 sc rnds = 1 inch

Pattern Notes

Weave in loose ends as work progresses.

Do not join rounds unless otherwise stated.

Use stitch marker to mark rounds, move marker as work progresses.

Hat
Crown

Rnd 1: With jute, ch 4, sl st in first ch to form a ring, ch 1, 6 sc in ring, place stitch marker. *(6 sc)*

Rnd 2: 2 sc in each sc around. *(12 sc)*

Rnd 3: [Sc in next sc, 2 sc in next sc] 6 times. *(18 sc)*

Rnd 4: [Sc in each of next 2 sc, 2 sc in next sc] 6 times. *(24 sc)*

Rnd 5: [Sc in each of next 3 sc, 2 sc in next sc] 6 times. *(30 sc)*

Rnd 6: [Sc in each of next 4 sc, 2 sc in next sc] 6 times. *(36 sc)*

Rnd 7: [Sc in each of next 5 sc, 2 sc in next sc] 6 times. *(42 sc)*

Rnd 8: [Sc in each of next 6 sc, 2 sc in next sc] 6 times. *(48 sc)*

Rnd 9: [Sc in each of next 7 sc, 2 sc in next sc] 6 times. *(54 sc)*

Rnd 10: [Sc in each of next 8 sc, 2 sc in next sc] 6 times. *(60 sc)*

Rnd 11: [Sc in each of next 9 sc, 2 sc in next sc] 6 times. *(66 sc)*

Rnd 12: [Sc in each of next 10 sc, 2 sc in next sc] 6 times. *(72 sc)*

Rnd 13: Working in **back lp** *(see Stitch Guide)* of each st, sc in each st around. *(72 sc)*

Rnd 14: Sc in each sc around.

Rnds 15–21: Rep rnd 14.

Rnd 22: [Sc in each of next 9 sc, ch 1, sk next sc, sc in next sc, ch 1, sk next sc] 6 times. *(60 sc, 12 ch-1 sps)*

Brim

Rnd 23: Working in **front lp** *(see Stitch Guide)* of each st, sc in each st around. *(72 sc)*

Rnd 24: [Sc in each of next 5 sc, 2 sc in next sc] 12 times. *(84 sc)*

Rnd 25: [Sc in each of next 6 sc, 2 sc in next sc] 12 times. *(96 sc)*

Rnds 26–29: Sc in each sc around.

Rnd 30: Sl st in each st around. Fasten off.

Tie

Row 1: With cornflower, ch 115. Fasten off.

Weaving Tie through rnd 22 of Crown, [insert Tie through RS into ch-1 sp to WS under sc and out through next ch-1 sp to RS] around, knot ends of Tie loosely.

Fly

Holding cornflower and jute tog, wrap around two fingers loosely 4 times. Cut ends. With care, remove wrap from fingers. With 5-inch length each cornflower and jute, pass through center of strands, knot ends to secure. Wrap a length of cornflower approximately ⅜ inch below top knotted section. Cut ends at bottom edge. Fray yarn ends slightly. Secure Fly to rnd 13 of Crown. ●

Bear Diaper Cover & Cap

Designs by Michele Wilcox

Skill Level

⬤⬤⬤◻ INTERMEDIATE

Finished Sizes

Newborn–3 months, 3–6 months and
9 months–1 year

Materials

- Cascade Fixation fine (sport) weight
  elastic yarn (1¾ oz/
  100 yds/50g per ball):
    2 balls #9442 hawaiian splendor
    1 ball each #7382 chocolate,
       #8176 ecru and #8001 opulent white
- Size 8 pearl cotton:
    10 yds each blue, black and brown
- Size crochet hook needed
  for size and gauge
- Tapestry needle
- Stitch marker

Gauge

Newborn–3 months, size C/2/2.75mm hook:
7 dc = 1 inch
3–6 months, size D/3/3.25mm hook:
6 dc = 1 inch
9 months–1 year, size E/4/3.5mm hook:
5 dc = 1 inch
Take time to check gauge.

Pattern Notes

If using a different yarn, make sure it will
stretch and also hold original shape and size,
in order to fit properly over diaper.

Chain-2 at beginning of row or round
counts as first double crochet unless
otherwise stated.

Work in continuous rounds, do not turn or
join unless otherwise stated.

Mark first stitch of each round.

Join with slip stitch as indicated unless
otherwise stated.

Diaper Cover
Back
Ribbing

Row 1: With hawaiian splendor, ch 9, sc in 2nd ch from hook and in each ch across, turn. *(8 sc)*

Rows 2–54: Working in **back lps** *(see Stitch Guide)*, ch 1, sc in each st across, turn. At end of last row, **do not turn.**

Body

Row 1: Working in ends of rows on Ribbing, ch 1, sc in each row across, turn. *(54 sc)*

Row 2: Working in both lps, ch 1, sc in each of first 8 sts, 2 sc in next st, [sc in each of next 8 sts, 2 sc in next st] across, turn. *(60 sc)*

Row 3: Ch 2 *(see Pattern Notes)*, dc in each st across, turn.

Row 4: Ch 1, sc in each st across, turn.

Rows 5–14: [Rep rows 3 and 4 alternately] 5 times.

Row 15: Rep row 3.

Row 16: Sk first st, loosely sl st in each of next 2 sts, sc in each of next 54 sts, leaving last 3 sts unworked, turn. *(54 sc)*

Rows 17–23: Sk first st, loosely sl st in each of next 2 sts, sc in each st across, leaving last 3 sc unworked, turn. *(12 sc at end of last row)*

Rows 24–32: Ch 1, sc in each st across, turn. At end of last row, fasten off.

Front
Ribbing

Row 1: With hawaiian splendor, ch 9, sc in 2nd ch from hook and in each ch across, turn. *(8 sc)*

Rows 2–18: Working in back lps, ch 1, sc in each st across, turn. At end of last row, **do not turn.**

Body

Row 1: Working in ends of rows on Ribbing, ch 1, sc in each row across, turn. *(18 sc)*

Row 2: Ch 1, sc in each of first 5 sts, 2 sc in next st, [sc in each of next 5 sts, 2 sc in next st] across, turn. Fasten off. *(21 sc)*

Row 3: Join *(see Pattern Notes)* opulent white in first st, ch 2, dc in each st across, turn.

Rows 4–12: [Rep rows 4 and 3 of Back Body alternately] 5 times, ending last rep with row 4. At end of last row, fasten off.

Row 13: Join hawaiian splendor in first st, ch 2, dc in each st across, turn.

Row 14: Rep row 4 of Back

Row 15: Rep row 3 of Back.

Row 16: Ch 1, sc in each st across, turn.

Row 17: Ch 1, **sc dec** *(see Stitch Guide)* in first 2 sts, sc in each st across, ending with sc dec in last 2 sts, turn. *(19 sc)*

Row 18: Ch 1, sc in each st across, turn.

Rows 19–24: [Rep rows 17 and 18 alternately] 3 times. *(13 sc at end of last row)*

Row 25: Ch 1, sc in each of first 6 sts, sc dec in next 2 sts, sc in each st across, turn. *(12 sc)*

Rows 26–32: Ch 1, sc in each st across, turn. At end of last row, fasten off.

Assembly

Sew side edges of Front to Back from Ribbing to top of row 16 of Body.

Sew last row of Front and Back tog for crotch.

Leg

Rnd 1: With hawaiian splendor, evenly sp 54 sc around Leg opening, **do not join** *(see Pattern Notes).*

Rnd 2: Sc in each st around.

Rnd 3: [Sc in each of next 7 sts, sc dec in next 2 sts] around. *(48 sc)*

Rnd 4: [Sc in each of next 6 sts, sc dec in next 2 sts] around. *(42 sc)*

Rnds 5 & 6: Sc in each st around. At end of last rnd, fasten off.

Rep on Leg opening.

Bear
Head

Rnd 1: With chocolate, ch 2, 6 sc in 2nd ch from hook, **do not join**. *(6 sc)*

Rnd 2: 2 sc in each st around. *(12 sc)*

Rnd 3: [Sc in next st, 2 sc in next st] around. *(18 sc)*

Rnd 4: [Sc in each of next 2 sts, 2 sc in next st] around. *(24 sc)*

Rnd 5: [Sc in each of next 3 sts, 2 sc in next st] around, join in next st. Fasten off. *(30 sc)*

Snout

Rnd 1: With ecru, ch 2, 6 sc in 2nd ch from hook, **do not join**. *(6 sc)*

Rnd 2: 2 sc in each st around, join in next st. Fasten off. *(12 sc)*

Ear

Make 2.
Row 1: With chocolate, ch 2, 5 sc in 2nd ch from hook, turn. *(5 sc)*

Row 2: 2 sc in each st across. Fasten off. *(10 sc)*

Assembly

Using **satin stitch** *(see illustration)*, with brown pearl cotton, embroider nose on Snout as shown in photo.

Using **straight stitch** *(see illustration)*, with brown pearl cotton, embroider mouth to Snout centered below nose as shown in photo.

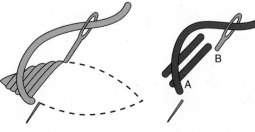

Satin Stitch   **Straight Stitch**

Sew Snout to Head as shown in photo.

Using **French knots** *(see illustration)*, with blue pearl cotton, embroider eyes on Head above Snout as shown in photo.

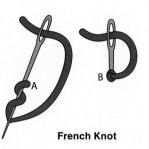

French Knot

Sew Head to white section on Front of Diaper Cover as shown in photo.

Sew 1 Ear to each side of Head as shown in photo.

Hat
Ribbing

Row 1: With hawaiian splendor, ch 13, sc in 2nd ch from hook and in each ch across, turn. *(12 sc)*

Rows 2–78: Working in **back lps** *(see Stitch Guide)*, ch 1, sc in each st across, turn. At end of last row, **do not turn**.

Top Section

Row 1: Working in ends of rows, ch 1, sc in each row across, turn. Fasten off. *(78 sc)*

Row 2: Join chocolate in first st, **ch 2** *(see Pattern Notes)*, dc in each st across, turn.

Row 3: Ch 1, sc in each st across, turn.

Rows 4–11: [Rep rows 2 and 3 alternately] 4 times.

Row 12: Ch 2, dc in each of next 10 sts, **dc dec** *(see Stitch Guide)* in next 2 sts, [dc in each of next 11 sts, dc dec in next 2 sts] across, turn. *(72 dc)*

Row 13: Ch 1, sc in each of first 10 sts, **sc dec** *(see Stitch Guide)* in next 2 sts, [sc in each of next 10 sts, sc dec in next 2 sts] across, turn. *(66 sc)*

Row 14: Ch 2, dc in each of next 8 sts, dc dec in next 2 sts, [dc in each of next 9 sts, dc dec in next 2 sts] across, turn. *(60 dc)*

Row 15: Ch 1, sc in each of first 8 sts, sc dec in next 2 sts, [sc in each of next 8 sts, sc dec in next 2 sts] across, turn. *(54 sc)*

Row 16: Ch 2, dc in each of next 6 sts, dc dec in next 2 sts, [dc in each of next 7 sts, dc dec in next 2 sts] across, turn. *(48 dc)*

Row 17: Ch 1, sc in each of first 6 sts, sc dec in next 2 sts, [sc in each of next 6 sts, sc dec in next 2 sts] across, turn. *(42 sc)*

Row 18: Ch 2, dc in each of next 4 sts, dc dec in next 2 sts, [dc in each of next 5 sts, dc dec in next 2 sts] across, turn. *(36 dc)*

Row 19: Ch 1, sc in each of first 4 sts, sc dec in next 2 sts, [sc in each of next 4 sts, sc dec in next 2 sts] across, turn. *(30 sc)*

Row 20: Ch 2, dc in each of next 2 sts, dc dec in next 2 sts, [dc in each of next 3 sts, dc dec in next 2 sts] across, turn. *(24 dc)*

Row 21: Ch 1, sc in each of first 2 sts, sc dec in next 2 sts, [sc in each of next 2 sts, sc dec in next 2 sts] across, turn. *(18 sc)*

Row 22: Ch 2, dc dec in next 2 sts, [dc in next st, dc dec in next 2 sts] across, turn. *(12 dc)*

Row 23: Ch 1, [sc dec in next 2 sts] across. Leaving long end, fasten off. *(6 sc)*

Weave long end through top of sts on last row, pull to close. Secure end.

Sew ends of rows tog for back seam.

Ear
Make 2.
Row 1: With chocolate, ch 2, 5 sc in 2nd ch from hook, turn. *(5 sc)*

Row 2: Ch 2, dc in same st, 2 dc in each st across, turn. *(10 dc)*

Row 3: Ch 1, sc in first st, 2 sc in next st, [sc in next st, 2 sc in next st] across, turn. *(15 sc)*

Row 4: Ch 2, dc in next st, 2 dc in next st, [dc in each of next 2 sts, 2 dc in next st] across, turn. *(20 dc)*

Row 5: Working in back lps, ch 1, sc in each st across, turn.

Row 6: Ch 2, dc in next st, dc dec in next 2 sts, [dc in each of next 2 sts, dc dec in next 2 sts] across, turn. *(15 dc)*

Row 7: [Sc in next st, sc dec in next 2 sts] across, turn. *(10 sc)*

Row 8: Ch 1, dc dec in first 2 sts, [dc dec in next 2 sts] across, turn. *(5 dc)*

Row 9: Ch 1, sc dec in next 5 sts. Leaving long end, fasten off.

Fold Ear in half and sew Ears to Top Section of Hat as shown in photo.

Snout
Rnd 1: With ecru, ch 2, 6 sc in 2nd ch from hook, **do not join.** *(6 sc)*

Rnd 2: 2 sc in each st around. *(12 sc)*

Rnd 3: [Sc in next st, 2 sc in next st] around. *(18 sc)*

Rnd 4: [Sc in each of next 2 sts, 2 sc in next st] around. *(24 sc)*

Rnd 5: [Sc in each of next 3 sts, 2 sc in next st] around. *(30 sc)*

Rnd 6: [Sc in each of next 4 sts, 2 sc in next st] around. *(36 sc)*

Rnd 7: [Sc in each of next 5 sts, 2 sc in next st] around, join in next st. Fasten off. *(42 sc)*

Finishing
Using satin stitch, with brown pearl cotton, embroider nose on Snout as shown in photo.

Using straight stitch, with brown pearl cotton, embroider mouth on Snout as shown in photo.

Sew Snout in place on Top Section of Hat between Ears.

Using satin stitch, with blue pearl cotton, embroider eyes above and on each side of Snout.

Using French knot, with black, embroider 1 French knot to top of each eye as shown in photo. •

Baby Hats

Designs by Nancy Nehring

Skill Level

■■■□ INTERMEDIATE

Finished Sizes

Instructions given fit newborn (16 inches circumference); changes for size 9 months (18 inches circumference) and toddler (20 inches circumference) are in [ ].

Materials

- Red Heart Soft Yarn medium (worsted) weight yarn (5 oz/256 yds/140g per ball):
  1 ball each #6768 pink (girl) (MC) and #4601 off-white (boy) (MC)
- Red Heart Baby Clouds super bulky (super chunky) weight yarn (6 oz/140 yds/170g per skein):
  3 oz #9311 cloud (CC)
- Size I/9/5.5mm crochet hook or size needed to obtain gauge
- Size N/13/9mm crochet hook
- Yarn needle
- Stitch markers

Gauge

Size I hook: 19 sts = 4 inches; 13 rows = 2 inches

Pattern Notes

Weave in loose ends as work progresses.

Join with slip stitch as indicated unless otherwise stated.

Slip stitches are worked in **back loops** (see Stitch Guide) only unless otherwise stated.

It may be hard to find the loop where you should place the last slip stitch, it tends to sink into the fabric near the turn. Push your hook straight down just behind the front loops, and then push back, loop should pop onto hook.

Hats
Crown

Row 1: With size I hook and MC, ch 19 [21, 22], beg in 2nd ch from hook, sl st in back lp of each ch across, turn. (18 [20, 22] sts)

Row 2: Ch 1, sl st in back lp of each of next 16 [18, 20] sts, leaving last 2 sts unworked, turn. (16 [18, 20] sts)

Row 3: Ch 1, sl st in back lp of each of next 16 [18, 20] sts, turn. (16 [18, 20] sts)

Row 4: Ch 1, sl st in back lp of each of next 12 [14, 16] sts, leaving last 4 sts unworked, turn. (12 [14, 16] sts)

Row 5: Ch 1, sl st in back lp of each of next 12 [14, 16] sts, turn.

Row 6: Ch 1, sl st in back lp of each of next 6 [8, 10] sts, leaving last 6 sts unworked, turn. (6 [8, 10] sts)

Row 7: Ch 1, sl st in back lp of each of next 6 [8, 10] sts, turn.

Row 8: Ch 1, sl st in back lp of each of next 18 [20, 22] sts, working the first 6 [8, 10] sts in row 7, the next 6 sts in row 5, the next 4 sts in row 3 and the last 2 sts in row 1, turn.

Row 9: Ch 1, sl st in back lp of each of next 18 [20, 22] sts, turn.

Rows 10–96 [10–104, 10–112]: [Rep rows 2–9 consecutively] 11 [12, 13] times, ending last rep with row 8.

Row 97 [105, 113]: Holding opposite side of foundation ch to row 96 [104, 112] and working through both thicknesses, ch 1, sl st in each st across. Fasten off.

Thread length of MC on yarn needle, weave through rem sts at top opening of Hat, draw ends tog to close opening, secure. Fasten off.

Tassel

Wrap MC around 3 fingers 20 times. With 6-inch length of MC, tie tightly in center of strands, with rem ends, pass through center top of Hat and secure on inside edge. Trim.

Ear Flaps

Make 2.
Note: Divide opening of Hat into quarters with seam at center back and mark with stitch markers. Center Ear Flaps and Front Flap over other three stitch markers.

Row 1: With size I hook and MC, ch 11 [13, 13], beg in 2nd ch from hook, sl st in back lp of each of next 10 [12, 12] chs, turn. *(10 [12, 12] sts)*

Rows 2–12 [2–12, 2–14]: Ch 1, sl st in back lp of each of next 10 [12, 12] sts, leaving last 2 sts unworked, turn. *(10 [12, 12] sts)*

At the end of row 12 [12, 14], do not fasten off.

Center Ear Flap over stitch marker with Ear Flap against WS of Hat and lining up ribs. Ball of yarn should be on starting edge. Insert hook through Hat and first st of Flap, sl st Hat and Flap tog in each valley of ribbing. Fasten off.

Front Flap

Row 1: With size N hook and CC, ch 10 [11, 11], sc in 2nd ch from hook, sc in each rem ch across, turn. *(9 [10, 10] sc)*

Rows 2 & 3 [2 & 3, 2–4]: Ch 1, sc in each sc across, turn. At the end of row 3 [3, 4], center Flap over center front on right side of Hat. Skein of yarn should be at starting edge, change to size I hook, insert through last lp of CC and through corresponding valley of rib of Hat, sl st across in every st of CC and as necessary in Hat, **do not fasten off**.

Continuing around Hat, sc in every valley of rib sts, in every other st along edge of Ear Flap, and 1 st in each outside corner of Ear Flap, ending with sl st in first sl st attaching Front Flap.

Front Flap Trim

With size I hook, attach MC to edge of Front Flap just above sl st, ch 1, working over CC yarn around 3 sides of Front Flap, working 2 sc over each row end, 5 sc in outer corner, 2 sc in each sc along top edge of Front Flap, 5 sc in outer corner, 2 sc over each row to next sl st. Fasten off.

With length of MC, tack upper corners of Front Flap to Hat. •

Flower Garden Ball

Design by Shirley Patterson

Skill Level

■■■□ INTERMEDIATE

Finished Size

Circumference: 19 inches

Materials

- Red Heart Soft Baby light (light worsted) weight yarn (solids: 7 oz/575 yds/198g; multis: 6 oz/430 yds/170g per skein):
  1 skein each #7001 white, #7737 powder pink, #7881 powder blue, #7680 new mint, #7321 powder yellow, #7588 lilac and #7964 naptime multi
- Size F/5/3.75mm crochet hook or size needed to obtain gauge
- Tapestry needle
- Fiberfill

Gauge

5 sc = 1 inch; 5 sc rnds = 1 inch

Pattern Notes

Weave in loose ends as work progresses.

Join with slip stitch as indicated unless otherwise stated.

Ball
Flower

Make 3 each powder pink, powder blue, powder yellow and lilac.

Rnd 1 (RS): Ch 3, **join** (see Pattern Notes) in first ch to form a ring, sl st in ring, [ch 13, sl st in ring, ch 9, sl st in ring, ch 7, sl st in ring, ch 9, sl st in ring] twice. Fasten off. (8 petals)

Cone Top

Make 12.

Row 1: With new mint, ch 2, sc in 2nd ch from hook, turn. (1 sc)

Row 2: Ch 1, 2 sc in next sc, turn. (2 sc)

Row 3: Ch 1, 2 sc in first sc, sc in next sc, turn. (3 sc)

Row 4: Ch 1, 2 sc in first sc, sc in each rem sc across, turn. (4 sc)

Rows 5–7: Rep row 4. (7 sc)

Rows 8 & 9: Ch 1, sc in each sc across, turn.

Row 10: Ch 1, **sc dec** (see Stitch Guide) in next 2 sc, sc in each rem sc across, turn. (6 sc)

Rows 11–13: Rep row 10. (3 sc)

Row 14: Ch 1, sc dec in next 2 sc, sc in next sc, turn. (2 sc)

Row 15: Ch 1, sc dec in next 2 sc, turn. (1 sc)

Rnd 16: Now working in rnds around the outer edge of Cone Top, connecting Flower to Cone Top and using care that Flower petals are at proper position, ch 1, sc in same sc as row 15, sc in each of next 3 sc, position Flower on top of Cone Top with a ch-13 pointing to top *(ch-13 at 12 o'clock)*, working in next st and ch-9 lp, sc in next st, sc in each of next 3 sts, sc in next st and over ch-7 lp *(ch-7 lp at 9 o'clock)*, sc in each of next 3 sts, sc in next st and ch-9 lp, sc in each of next 3 sts, sc in bottom of row 1, sc in same st and over next ch-13 lp *(ch-13 at 6 o'clock)*, work 1 more sc in same st *(3 sc in opposite side of foundation ch of row 1)*, sc in each of next 3 sts, sc in next sc and next ch-9 lp, sc in each of next 3 sc, sc in next st and over ch-7 lp *(ch-7 lp at 3 o'clock)*, sc in each of next 3 sts, sc in next st and ch-9 lp, sc in each of next 3 sts, sc in next sc *(row 15)*, sc in same sc and in rem ch-13 lp *(12 o'clock)*, join in beg sc. Fasten off. *(36 sc)*

Rnd 17: Working in **front lps** *(see Stitch Guide)* of sc sts of rnd 16, join white in any st, sl st in each st around. Fasten off. *(36 sl sts)*

Cone Bottom

Rnd 1: Working in **back lps** *(see Stitch Guide)* of rnd 16, join naptime multi in sc in line with ch-13 lp, ch 1, sc in each st around, join in beg sc. *(36 sc)*

Rnd 2: Ch 1, sc in each of next 9 sc, sc dec in next 2 sc, sc in each of next 15 sc, sc dec in next 2 sc, sc in each of next 8 sc, join in beg sc. *(34 sc)*

Rnd 3: Ch 1, sc in each of next 8 sc, sc dec in next 2 sc, sc in each of next 14 sc, sc dec in next 2 sc, sc in each of next 8 sc, join in beg sc. *(32 sc)*

Rnd 4: Ch 1, sc in each of next 7 sc, sc dec in next 2 sc, sc in each of next 13 sc, sc dec in next 2 sc, sc in each of next 8 sc, join in beg sc. *(30 sc)*

Rnd 5: Ch 1, sc in each of next 6 sc, sc dec in next 2 sc, sc in each of next 12 sc, sc dec in next 2 sc, sc in each of next 8 sc, join in beg sc. *(28 sc)*

Rnd 6: Ch 1, sc in each of next 5 sc, sc dec in next 2 sc, sc in each of next 11 sc, sc dec in next 2 sc, sc in each of next 8 sc, join in beg sc. *(26 sc)*

Rnd 7: Ch 1, sc in each of next 4 sc, sc dec in next 2 sc, sc in each of next 10 sc, sc dec in next 2 sc, sc in each of next 8 sc, join in beg sc. *(24 sc)*

Rnd 8: Ch 1, sc in each of next 3 sc, sc dec in next 2 sc, sc in each of next 9 sc, sc dec in next 2 sc, sc in each of next 8 sc, join in beg sc. *(22 sc)*

Rnd 9: Ch 1, sc in each of next 2 sc, sc dec in next 2 sc, sc in each of next 8 sc, sc dec in next 2 sc, sc in each of next 8 sc, join in beg sc. *(20 sc)*

Rnd 10: Ch 1, sc in next sc, sc dec in next 2 sc, sc in each of next 7 sc, sc dec in next 2 sc, sc in each of next 8 sc, join in beg sc. *(18 sc)*

Rnd 11: Ch 1, sc dec in next 2 sc, sc in each of next 6 sc, sc dec in next 2 sc, sc in each of next 8 sc, join in beg sc. *(16 sc)*

Rnd 12: Ch 1, [draw up a lp in each of next 3 sc, yo, draw through all 4 lps on hook] 5 times, sc in next sc, join in beg sc. *(6 sc)*

Stuff Cone Bottom with fiberfill.

Row 13: Now working in rows, fold rnd 12 flat across, working through both thicknesses, work 3 sl sts across. Fasten off.

Finishing

Thread 18-inch length of yarn on tapestry needle. Holding 1 of each Flower color tog at base of Cones, thread yarn through last rnd of the 4 Cones, pull tight and secure. Weave a strand of yarn through center sl st at each point of rnd 17 at the 4 points *(in line with ch-13 lp points)*, pull tight, secure and fasten off.

Thread another 2nd 4-Cone grouping in same manner as first group. Place on top of first group, having points of Cone to fit lengthwise to points of first 4-Cone group in diameter position. Continue with 3rd 4-Cone group in same manner as first 4-Cone group. Lay on top of 2nd 4-Cone group so that it lies in the same position as the first 4-Cone group. Secure points of last 4-Cone group in same manner as first 4-Cone group, matching 2nd 4-cone group to other unworked points. Secure all points of 4. ●

Pig Security Blanket

Design by Helen Heaverin

Skill Level

■■□□ EASY

Finished Sizes

Blanket: 12 inches square
Pig: 2½ inches tall

Materials

- Caron Simply Soft Brites medium (worsted) weight yarn (6 oz/315 yds/170g per skein): 1 skein #9604 watermelon
- Caron Simply Soft medium (worsted) weight yarn (6 oz/315 yds/170g per skein): 1 skein #9719 soft pink
- 1 yd black medium (worsted) weight yarn
- Sizes F/5/3.75mm and H/8/5mm crochet hooks or sizes needed to obtain gauge
- Tapestry needle
- Fiberfill
- Stitch marker

Gauge

Size F hook: 5 sc = 1 inch; 5 sc rnds = 1 inch
Size H hook: 4 dc = 1 inch; 2 dc rnds = 1 inch

Pattern Notes

Weave in loose ends as work progresses.

Join with slip stitch as indicated unless otherwise stated.

Chain-3 at beginning of rounds counts as first double crochet unless otherwise stated.

Do not join rounds unless otherwise stated. Use stitch marker to mark rounds.

Special Stitches

Scallop: (5 dc) in indicated st.

Picot: Ch 2, sl st in 2nd ch from hook.

Pig Blanket

Blanket

Rnd 1: Starting at center with size H hook and watermelon, ch 4, **join** *(see Pattern Notes)* in first ch to form a ring, **ch 3** *(see Pattern Notes)*, 11 dc in ring, join in 3rd ch of beg ch-3. *(12 dc)*

Rnd 2: Ch 3, *(2 dc, tr) in next dc, (tr, 2 dc) in next dc**, dc in next dc, rep from * around, ending last rep at **, join in 3rd ch of ch-3. *(20 dc, 8 tr)*

Rnd 3: Ch 3, dc in each of next 2 dc, *(2 dc, tr) in next dc, (tr, 2 dc) in next dc**, dc in each of next 5 dc, rep from * around, ending last rep at **, dc in each of next 2 dc, join in 3rd ch of ch-3. *(36 dc, 8 tr)*

Rnd 4: Ch 3, dc in each of next 4 dc, *(2 dc, tr) in next dc, (tr, 2 dc) in next dc**, dc in each of next 9 dc, rep from * around, ending last rep at **, dc in each of next 4 dc, join in 3rd ch of ch-3. *(52 dc, 8 tr)*

Rnd 5: Ch 3, dc in each of next 6 dc, *(2 dc, tr) in next dc, (tr, 2 dc) in next dc**, dc in each of next 13 dc, rep from * around, ending last rep at **, dc in each of next 6 dc, join in 3rd ch of ch-3. *(68 dc, 8 tr)*

Rnd 6: Ch 3, dc in each of next 8 dc, *(2 dc, tr) in next dc, (tr, 2 dc) in next dc**, dc in each of next 17 dc, rep from * around, ending last rep at **, dc in each of next 8 dc, join in 3rd ch of ch-3. *(84 dc, 8 tr)*

Rnd 7: Ch 3, dc in each of next 10 dc, *(2 dc, tr) in next dc, (tr, 2 dc) in next dc**, dc in each of next 21 dc, rep from * around, ending last rep at **, dc in each of next 10 dc, join in 3rd ch of ch-3. *(100 dc, 8 tr)*

Rnd 8: Ch 3, dc in each of next 12 dc, *(2 dc, tr) in next dc, (tr, 2 dc) in next dc**, dc in each of next 25 dc, rep from * around, ending last rep at **, dc in each of next 12 dc, join in 3rd ch of ch-3. *(116 dc, 8 tr)*

Rnd 9: Ch 3, dc in each of next 14 dc, *(2 dc, tr) in next dc, (tr, 2 dc) in next dc**, dc in each of next 29 dc, rep from * around, ending last rep at **, dc in each of next 14 dc, join in 3rd ch of ch-3. *(132 dc, 8 tr)*

Rnd 10: Ch 3, dc in each of next 16 dc, *(2 dc, tr) in next dc, (tr, 2 dc) in next dc**, dc in each of next 33 dc, rep from * around, ending last rep at **, dc in each of next 16 dc, join in 3rd ch of ch-3. Fasten off. *(148 dc, 8 tr)*

Trim

Rnd 11: Working in **back lps** *(see Stitch Guide)*, join soft pink in joining of previous rnd, ch 1, sc in same st as beg ch-1, sc in each st around, join in first sc. *(156 sc)*

Rnd 12: Ch 1, sc in first sc, [sk next sc, **scallop** *(see Special Stitches)* in next sc, sk next sc, sc in next sc] around, join in beg sc. Fasten off. *(39 scallops)*

Head

Rnd 1: Starting at top of Head with size F hook and watermelon, make **slip ring** *(see illustration)*, 6 sc in 2nd ch from hook, tighten ring. *(6 sc)*

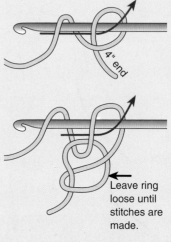

Leave ring loose until stitches are made.

Slip Ring

Rnd 2: 2 sc in each sc around. *(12 sc)*

Rnd 3: [2 sc in next sc, sc in next sc] around. *(18 sc)*

Rnd 4: [2 sc in next sc, sc in each of next 2 sc] around. *(24 sc)*

Rnd 5: [2 sc in next sc, sc in each of next 3 sc] around. *(30 sc)*

Rnd 6: Sc in each sc around.

Rnds 7–10: Rep rnd 6.

Rnd 11: [Sc dec *(see Stitch Guide)* in next 2 sc, sc in each of next 3 sc] around. *(24 sc)*

Rnd 12: [Sc dec in next 2 sc, sc in each of next 2 sc] around. *(18 sc)*

Stuff Head with fiberfill and continue stuffing as work progresses.

Rnd 13: [Sc dec in next 2 sc, sc in next sc] around. *(12 sc)*

Rnd 14: [Sc dec in next 2 sc] around. **Do not fasten off.** *(6 sc)*

Arm
Make 2.
Rnd 15: 2 sc in each of next 3 sc, leaving rem 3 sc for 2nd Arm. *(6 sc)*

Rnds 16 & 17: Rep rnd 6.

Rnd 18: Rep rnd 2. *(12 sc)*

Rnds 19 & 20: Rep rnd 6.

Rnd 21: Rep rnd 3. *(18 sc)*

Rnds 22 & 23: Rep rnd 6. At the end of rnd 23, fasten off.

Firmly stuff Arm with fiberfill.

Arm Closure
Make 2.
Rnd 1: With size F hook and soft pink, make slip ring, 6 sc in 2nd ch from hook, tighten ring. *(6 sc)*

Rnd 2: 2 sc in each sc around. *(12 sc)*

Rnd 3: [2 sc in next sc, sc in next sc] around. *(18 sc)*

Rnd 4: Working through both thicknesses of rnd 3 and **front lps** *(see Stitch Guide)* of rnd 23 of Arm, sc in each st around, join in beg sc. Fasten off.

Working in rem 3 sc of rnd 14 of Head, beg with rnd 15, rep for 2nd Arm.

Snout
Rnd 1: With size F hook and soft pink, make slip ring, 9 sc in ring, tighten ring. Leaving 6-inch length, fasten off.

With length of watermelon, for nostrils, sew 2 straight vertical lines on center front of Snout. Sew Snout to front of Head.

Outer Ear
Make 2.
Row 1: With size F hook and watermelon, make slip ring, 6 sc in ring, tighten slip ring, turn. *(6 sc)*

Row 2: Ch 1, sc dec in next 2 sc, sc in each of next 2 sc, sc dec in next 2 sc, turn. *(4 sc)*

Row 3: Ch 1, [sc dec in next 2 sc] twice, turn. *(2 sc)*

Row 4: Ch 1, sc dec in next 2 sc. Fasten off. *(1 sc)*

Inner Ear
Make 2.
Row 1: With size F hook and soft pink, make slip ring, 5 sc in ring, tighten slip ring, turn. *(5 sc)*

Row 2: Ch 1, sc dec in next 2 sc, sc in next sc, sc dec in next 2 sc, turn. *(3 sc)*

Row 3: Ch 1, sc dec in next 2 sc, sc in next sc, turn. *(2 sc)*

Row 4: Ch 1, sc dec in next 2 sc. Fasten off. *(1 sc)*

With length of watermelon, sew Inner Ear inside Outer Ear. Sew Ears to top of Head.

Finishing
With black, embroider 2 small sts on Head front slightly above Snout.

With length of watermelon, adjusting Arms as needed, sew Head to center of Blanket. ●

Nursing Pillow

Design by Darla Sims

Skill Level

■■■□ INTERMEDIATE

Finished Size

11¾ inches wide x 15½ inches long

Materials

- TLC Amoré medium (worsted) weight yarn (6 oz/335yds/170g per skein):
    1 skein each #3103 vanilla and #3005 sand
- TLC Baby Amoré medium (worsted) weight yarn (5 oz/279 yds/140g per skein):
    1 skein #9620 spearmint
- Sizes F/5/3.75mm and H/8/5mm crochet hooks or size needed to obtain gauge
- Tapestry needle
- Sewing needle and thread
- Straight pins
- Sewing machine (optional)
- 45-inch-wide fabric: ⅔ yd
- Fiberfill

Gauge

Size H hook: 7 sts = 2 inches

Pattern Notes

Weave in loose ends as work progresses.

Join with slip stitch as indicated unless otherwise stated.

Special Stitch

Picot: Ch 3, sl st in 3rd ch from hook.

Pillow

Pillow Side

Make 2.

Row 1 (RS): With size H hook and vanilla, ch 4, 2 sc in 2nd ch from hook, 2 sc in each of next 2 chs, turn. *(6 sc)*

Row 2: Ch 1, 2 hdc in each st across, turn. *(12 hdc)*

Row 3: Ch 1, hdc in each st across, turn.

Row 4: Ch 1, hdc in first st, 2 hdc in next st, [hdc in next st, 2 hdc in next st] across, turn. *(18 hdc)*

Row 5: Ch 1, 2 hdc in first st, hdc in each st across to last st, 2 hdc in last st, turn. *(20 hdc)*

Row 6: Rep row 3.

Row 7: Rep row 4. *(30 hdc)*

Row 8: Rep row 3.

Row 9: Ch 1, [hdc in each of next 2 hdc, 2 hdc in next hdc] across, turn. *(40 hdc)*

Rows 10 & 11: Rep row 3.

Row 12: Rep row 4. *(60 hdc)*

Rows 13–16: Rep row 3.

Row 17: Rep row 4. *(90 hdc)*

Rows 18–20: Rep row 3.

Row 21: Ch 1, hdc in first st, hdc in each of next 3 sts, 2 hdc in next st, [hdc in each of next 4 sts, 2 hdc in next st] across, turn. *(108 hdc)*

Rows 22 & 23: Rep row 3. At the end of last rep, fasten off.

Side Edging

Row 1 (RS): Working in posts of hdc sts of row 23, with size H hook, join spearmint with **fpsc** (see Stitch Guide) in first hdc post of row 23, [ch 3, fpsc in next hdc] across. Fasten off.

Gusset

Row 1: With size H hook and sand, ch 3, hdc in 3rd ch from hook, turn. *(2 hdc)*

Row 2: Ch 1, 2 hdc in each of next 2 hdc, turn. *(4 hdc)*

Row 3: Ch 1, hdc in each hdc across, turn.

Row 4: Ch 1, 2 hdc in first hdc, hdc in each hdc across to last hdc, 2 hdc in last hdc, turn. *(6 hdc)*

Rows 5–16: [Rep rows 3 and 4 alternately] 6 times. *(18 hdc)*

Rows 17–65: Rep row 3.

Row 66: Ch 1, **hdc dec** *(see Stitch Guide)* in next 2 hdc, hdc in each hdc across to last 2 hdc, hdc dec in next 2 hdc, turn. *(16 hdc)*

Row 67: Ch 1, hdc in each hdc across, turn.

Rows 68–79: [Rep rows 66 and 67 alternately] 6 times. *(4 hdc)*

Row 80: Ch 1, [hdc dec in next 2 hdc] twice, turn. *(2 hdc)*

Row 81: Rep row 67. Fasten off.

Edging

Rnd 1: With size H hook, join vanilla with sc in side edge of any row, sc evenly sp around, taking care to keep work flat, **join** *(see Pattern Notes)* in beg sc. Fasten off.

Fabric Pillow Form

Place Pillow Sides and Gusset on fabric, allowing ½-inch seam allowance around outer edge of each piece, draw around pieces, cutting 2 Pillow Sides and 1 Gusset.

With RS tog, sew Pillow sides and Gusset tog, leaving 6-inch opening, turn pillow right side out. Stuff pillow with fiberfill, sew opening closed.

Large Flower

Make 3 each sand and spearmint.
Rnd 1: With size F hook, ch 7, tr in 4th ch from hook, dc in next ch, hdc in next ch, sl st in last ch *(petal)*, [ch 6, tr in 4th ch from hook, dc in next ch, hdc in next ch, sl st in last ch] 4 times, join. Fasten off. *(5 petals)*

Medium Flower

Make 2 each sand and spearmint.
Rnd 1: With size F hook and vanilla, ch 2, 5 sc in 2nd ch from hook, join in first sc. Fasten off. *(5 sc)*

Rnd 2: Join Medium Flower color in any st, (ch 2, hdc, ch 2, sl st) in same st *(petal)*, [(sl st, ch 2, hdc, ch 2, sl st) in next st] 4 times, join in beg sl st. Fasten off. *(5 petals)*

Small Flower

Make 4 each sand and spearmint.
Rnd 1: With size F hook, ch 2, sl st in 2nd ch from hook, **picot** *(see Special Stitch)*, [sl st in beg 2nd ch from hook, picot] 4 times. Fasten off. *(5 petals)*

Sew Flowers as desired to one Pillow Side.

With RS of Pillow Sides and Gusset facing, with tapestry needle and length of vanilla, sew edges of Pillow Sides to Gusset. Turn RS out, insert pillow form and sew straight edge of Pillow Sides tog. •

cuddle baby

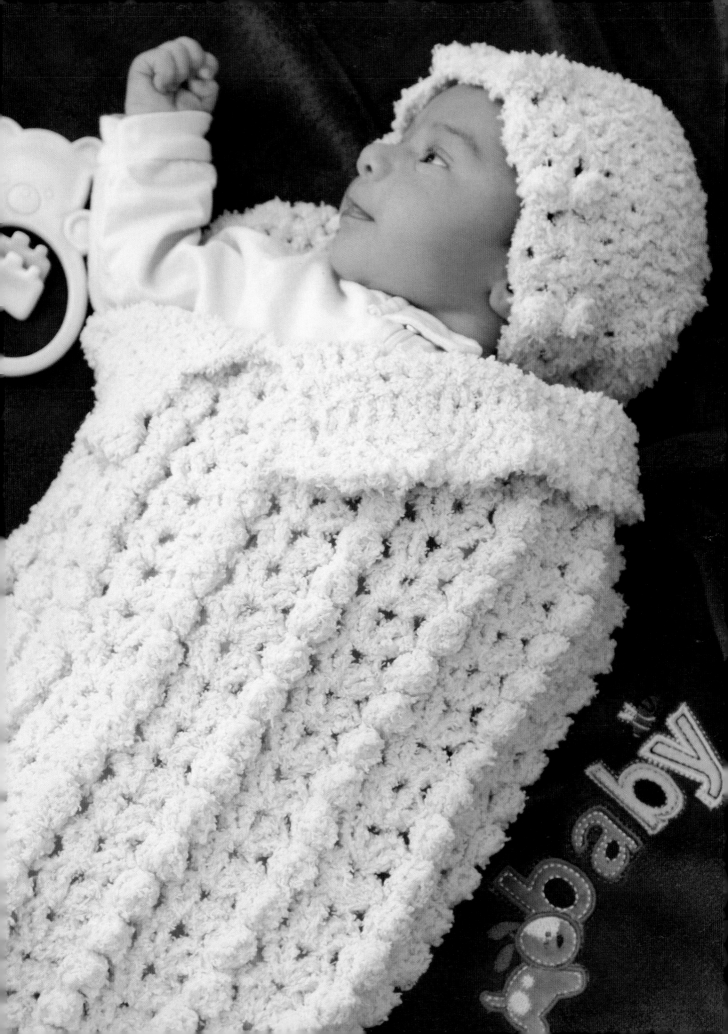

Little Lamb Set

Designs by Dorothy Warrell

Skill Level

INTERMEDIATE

Finished Sizes
Blanket: 24 x 38 inches without Border;
34 x 48 inches with Border
Pillow: 12 x 16 inches
Lamb: 10 inches

Materials

- Bernat Baby Coordinates light (light worsted) weight yarn (5½ oz/431 yds/ 160g per ball):
    4 balls #01012 iced mint *(A)*
    1 ball each #01000 white *(B)*, #01009 soft blue *(C)* and #01008 baby pink *(D)*
- Medium (worsted) weight yarn:
    1 oz white *(E)*
- Sizes F/5/3.75mm, G/6/4mm and H/8/5mm crochet hooks
- Size H/8/5mm flexible afghan crochet hook or size needed to obtain gauge
- Tapestry needle
- ⅝-inch-wide transparent white ribbon: 1 yd
- ⅞-inch-wide pink satin ribbon: 24 inches
- 12mm light blue buttons: 4
- 12 x 16-inch pillow form
- Fiberfill
- Stitch marker

Gauge
Size H afghan hook: 16 sts = 4 inches;
12½ rows = 4 inches

Pattern Notes
Weave in loose ends as work progresses.

Join with slip stitch as indicated unless otherwise stated.

Flowers are crocheted separately and sewn on Blanket.

Chain-3 at beginning of round counts as first double crochet unless otherwise indicated.

Do not join rounds, use stitch marker to mark beginning of round unless otherwise stated.

Special Stitches
Knot loop stitch (knot lp st): Work sc in rem lp, *draw up lp to measure 1 inch, draw yarn through long lp, sc between long lp and single strand, sc in next free lp.

Lamb loop stitch (lamb lp st): Draw up a lp under vertical bar of previous row, draw up a lp in vertical bar directly below in next row, yo, draw through 1 lp, yo, draw through 2 lps on hook, carry rem lp on hook.

Blanket
Body

Row 1: Working Blanket from top to bottom in **Afghan Stitch** *(see illustration)*, with size H afghan hook and A, ch 100, draw up lp in 2nd ch from hook and each rem ch across, retaining all lps on hook, yo, draw through first lp on hook, [yo, draw through 2 lps on hook] across until 1 lp remains and counts as first st of next row.

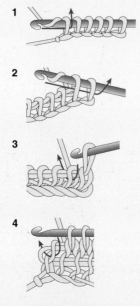

Afghan Stitch

Row 2: Draw up lp under first vertical bar of previous row, draw up lp in each vertical bar across, yo, draw through first lp on hook, [yo, draw through 2 lps on hook] across until 1 lp remains on hook.

Rows 3–40: Rep row 2.

Rows 41–80: Following chart and **changing colors** *(see Stitch Guide)* as color changes, work Lamb centered over Blanket, working **lamb lp st** *(see Special Stitches)* as indicated on chart as Pattern St.

Rows 81–125: Rep row 2.

Row 126: Sl st in each st across. Fasten off.

Border

Rnd 1: With size H hook, join A with sc in top right corner, sc in each st across top edge, 3 sc in next corner, sc in side edge of each row, 3 sc in corner, sc in each st across bottom edge, 3 sc in corner, sc in side edge of each row, 2 sc in same st as beg sc, **join** *(see Pattern Notes)* in first sc. Fasten off.

Rnd 2: Join B with sc in 7th sc from corner, *ch 3, sk next 2 sc, sc in next sc, turn, sc in each ch of ch-3 *(cable made)*, turn, with cable held forward, sc in each of 2 sk sc sts, rep from * to corner; [for corner, ch 3, sk 1 sc, sc in next sc, turn, sc in each of next 3 chs, sl st in sc of last cable, turn, with cable held forward, sc in same sc as sl st, sc in sk st] 3 times for corner, rep from * around, ending with ch 3, sc in same sc as beg sc, turn, sc in each ch of ch-3, sl st in sc, sc in 2 sk sc sts, sl st behind first cable. Fasten off.

Rnd 3: Join A to first sc of any 2 sc group worked behind cable, ch 1, sc in same sc, sc in next sc, ch 1, *[sc in each of next 2 sc, ch 1] across to next corner, at corner work sc in first corner sc, ch 1, 3 sc in center corner sc, ch 1, sc in last corner sc, ch 1, rep from * around, join in beg sc. Fasten off.

Rnd 4: Join B with sc in first sc of 3-sc corner, ch 2, sk center sc, sc in 3rd sc, ch 2, sc in next ch-1 sp, *[ch 2, sk next 2 sc, sc in next ch-1 sp] rep across to next corner, sc in first sc of corner, ch 2, sk center sc, sc in 3rd sc, ch 2, sc in next ch-1 sp, rep from * around, join in beg sc. Fasten off.

Rnd 5: Join A in corner ch-2 sp, **ch 3** *(see Pattern Notes)*, 5 dc in same ch-2 sp, *[3 dc in next ch-2 sp] across to next corner ch-2 sp, work 6 dc in corner ch-2 sp, rep from * around, join in 3rd ch of beg ch-3, draw up a lp, drop lp from hook, **do not fasten off**.

COLOR AND STITCH KEY
■ White
■ Baby pink
□ Soft blue
□ Iced mint for background
⊠ Pattern stitch
i Ribbon insert
◉ French Knot

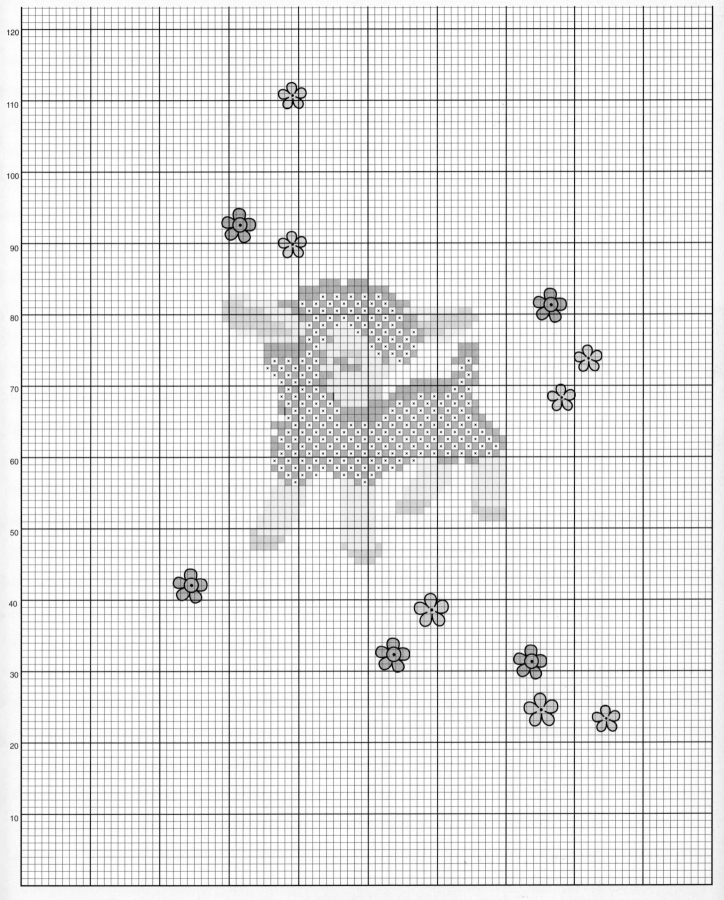

Little Lamb Crib Cover

Rnd 6: Join B with *sc between 2nd and 3rd dc of corner, ch 2, sc between 4th and 5th dc sts of corner, [ch 2, sc between next 3-dc groups] across, rep from * around, join in beg sc, draw up lp, drop lp from hook, **do not fasten off.**

Rnd 7: Pick up dropped lp of A, sl st in next ch-2 sp, ch 3, 2 dc in next ch-2 sp, *6 dc in corner ch-2 sp, [3 dc in next ch-2 sp] across to next corner, rep from * around, join in 3rd ch of beg ch-3, draw up lp, drop lp from hook, do not fasten off.

Rnd 8: Pick up dropped lp of B, *sc between 2nd and 3rd dc of corner, ch 2, sc between 4th and 5th dc sts of corner, [ch 2, sc between next 3 dc groups] across, rep from * around, join in beg sc, draw up lp, drop lp from hook, **do not fasten off.**

Rnds 9–12: [Rep rnds 6 and 7 alternately] twice.

Rnd 13: Rep rnd 6.

Rnd 14: Join white in corner, ch 1, [sl st in next st, ch 1] around, join in first sl st. Fasten off.

Small Flower
Make 7.
Rnd 1: With size F hook and D, wrap yarn around index finger twice to form ring, sl st in ring, [ch 3, 2 dc in ring, sl st in ring] 5 times. Leaving 10-inch length, fasten off. Draw rem beg length to close ring. *(5 petals)*

Medium Flower
Make 5.
Rnd 1: With size F hook and B, wrap yarn around finger twice, sl st in ring, ch 1, 20 sc in ring, join in beg sc.

Rnd 2: [Ch 3, dc in each of next 2 sc, sl st in each of next 2 sc] 5 times, ending with sl st in last sc. Leaving 10-inch length, fasten off. *(5 petals)*

Arrange Flowers according to chart. With rem length, tack petals on outer edges. With tapestry needle and length of A, embroider a **French knot** *(see illustration)* in center of each Flower.

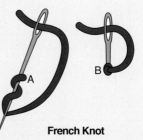

French Knot

Finishing
For eye, sew button as indicated to Lamb. To avoid choking hazard of young children, with light blue yarn, ch 2, 5 sc in 2nd ch from hook, leaving 5 inch length of yarn, **join** *(see Pattern Notes)* in beg sc. Sew crocheted eyes in place.

Cut 20-inch length of clear ribbon, insert ends from back to front through openings between sts. Tie ribbon ends in bow at front, trim ends as desired.

Pillow
Back

Row 1: With size H afghan hook and A, ch 64, draw up lp in 2nd ch from hook and each rem ch across retaining all lps on hook, yo, draw through first lp on hook, [yo, draw through 2 lps on hook] across until 1 lp remains and counts as first st of next row.

Row 2: Draw up lp under first vertical bar of previous row, draw up lp in each vertical bar across, yo, draw through first lp on hook, [yo, draw through 2 lps on hook] across until 1 lp remains on hook.

Rows 3–38: Rep row 2.

Row 39: Sl st in each st across, **do not fasten off.**

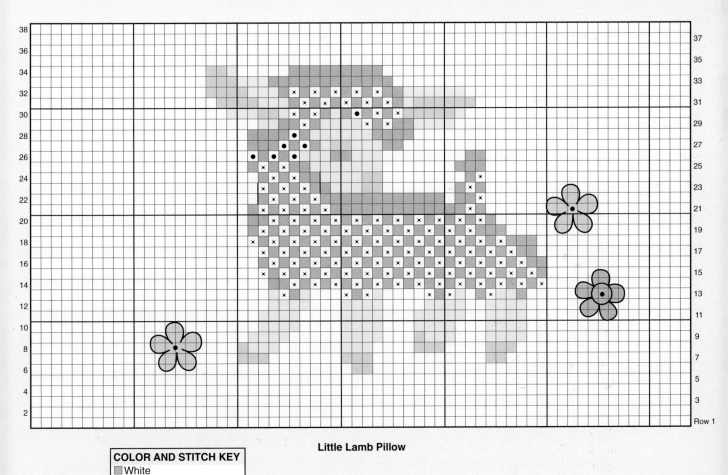

Little Lamb Pillow

COLOR AND STITCH KEY
- ▨ White
- ▨ Baby pink
- ▨ Soft blue
- ☐ Iced mint for background
- ⊠ Pattern stitch
- Ⅰ Ribbon insert
- ● French Knot

Border

Rnd 1: Ch 1, work 3 sc in each corner, 61 sc across each top and bottom of Back and 37 sc in ends of rows across each end, **join** (see Pattern Notes) in beg sc. Fasten off.

Front

Row 1: With size H afghan hook and A, ch 64, draw up lp in 2nd ch from hook and each rem ch across retaining all lps on hook, yo, draw through first lp on hook, [yo, draw through 2 lps on hook] across until 1 lp remains and counts as first st of next row.

Row 2: Draw up lp under first vertical bar of previous row, draw up lp in each vertical bar across, yo, draw through first lp on hook, [yo, draw through 2 lps on hook] across until 1 lp remains on hook.

Rows 3–38: Following chart and **changing colors** (see Stitch Guide) as color changes, work Lamb centered over Pillow, working **lamb lp st** (see Special Stitches) as indicated on chart as Pattern St.

Row 39: Sl st in each st across, **do not fasten off**.

Border

Rnd 1: Ch 1, work 3 sc in each corner, 61 sc across each top and bottom of Back and 37 sc in ends of rows across each end, join in beg sc. Fasten off.

Rnd 2: Join B with sc in 7th sc from corner, *ch 3, sk next 2 sc, sc in next sc, turn, sc in each ch of ch-3 (cable made), turn, with cable held forward, sc in each of 2 sk sc sts, rep from * to corner; [for corner, ch 3, sk 1 sc, sc in next sc, turn, sc in each of next 3 chs, sl st in sc of last cable, turn, with cable held forward, sc in same sc as sl st, sc in sk st] 3 times for corner, rep from * around, ending with ch 3, sc in same sc as beg sc, turn, sc in each ch of ch-3, sl st in sc, sc in 2 sk sc, sl st behind first cable. Fasten off.

Rnd 3: Join A to first sc of any 2 sc group worked behind cable, ch 1, sc in same sc, sc in next sc, ch 1, *[sc in each of next 2 sc, ch 1]

across to next corner, at corner work sc in first corner sc, ch 1, 3 sc in center corner sc, ch 1, sc in last corner sc, ch 1, rep from * around, join in beg sc. Fasten off.

Rnd 4: Holding Front and Back tog, working through both thicknesses, join B in lower left corner, ch 1, [sl st in next st, ch 1] around, inserting pillow form before closing. Fasten off.

Small Flower
Make 2.

Rnd 1: With size F hook and D, wrap yarn around index finger twice to form ring, sl st in ring, [ch 3, 2 dc in ring, sl st in ring] 5 times. Leaving 10-inch length, fasten off. Draw rem beg length to close ring. (5 petals)

Medium Flower
Make 1.

Rnd 1: With size F hook and B, wrap yarn around finger twice, sl st in ring, ch 1, 20 sc in ring, join in beg sc.

Rnd 2: [Ch 3, dc in each of next 2 sc, sl st in each of next 2 sc] 5 times, ending with sl st in last sc. Leaving 10-inch length, fasten off. (5 petals)

Arrange Flowers according to chart. With rem length, tack petals on outer edges. With tapestry needle and length of A, embroider a French knot in center of each Flower.

Finishing

For eye, sew button as indicated to Lamb. To avoid choking hazard of young children, with light blue yarn, ch 2, 5 sc in 2nd ch from hook, leaving 5-inch length of yarn, **join** (see Pattern Notes) in beg sc. Sew crocheted eyes in place.

For younger children do not use ribbon or use care to double knot ribbon to avoid removal of ribbon.

Cut 16-inch length of clear ribbon, insert ends from back to front through openings between sts. Tie ribbon ends in bow at front, trim ends as desired.

Lamb

Body

Rnd 1: Beg at back of Body, with size G hook and E, ch 2, 7 sc in 2nd ch from hook, do not join, place st marker. *(7 sc)*

Rnd 2: Working in **back lp** *(see Stitch Guide)*, 2 sc in each sc around. *(14 sc)*

Note: *Work in back lps of each st throughout unless otherwise indicated. Knot lp st will be worked in front lp later.*

Rnd 3: [Sc in next sc, 2 sc in next sc] around, **join** *(see Pattern Notes)* in beg sc. *(21 sc)*

Rnds 4–8: Ch 3 *(see Pattern Notes)*, dc in each of next 20 sts, join in 3rd ch of beg ch-3. *(21 dc)*

Neck Shaping

Rnd 1: Working in back lps, [**sc dec** *(see Stitch Guide)* in next 2 sts, sc in each of next 2 sts] 4 times, sc dec in next 2 sts, sc in next st, sc dec in next 2 sts, do not join. *(15 sc)*

Rnd 2: [Sc in each of next 3 sc, sc dec in next 2 sc] 3 times. *(12 sc)*

Rnds 3–5: Hdc in first st, dc in each of next 4 sts, hdc in each of next 2 sts, sc in each of next 4 sts, hdc in next st. *(12 sts)*

Row 6: Now working in rows, 2 sc in each of next 6 sts, leaving rem sts unworked, turn. *(12 sc)*

Row 7: Ch 1, working in both lps, sc in each of next 12 sc *(back of neck)*. Fasten off.

Body Loops

With size G hook, join B in first free lp on rnd 1 of Body, sc in same st as beg sl st, *****knot lp st** *(see Special Stitches)* in next st, sc in next st, rep from * over entire body, ending with sc in last st. Fasten off.

With fiberfill, stuff Body lightly.

Head

Rnd 1: With size G hook, join C in first st at top of back of neck, ch 1, sc in same st as beg ch-1, sc in next st, ch 8 *(for ear)*, sc in 2nd ch from hook, sc in next ch, hdc in each of next 2 chs, dc in each of next 3 chs, sc in each of next 8 sts on back of neck, ch 8 *(for ear)*, sc in 2nd ch from hook, sc in next ch, hdc in each of next 2 chs, dc in each of next 3 chs, sc in each of next 2 sts on back of neck, 1 sc on side edge of row below, sc in each rem 6 sts at base of neck *(rnd 5 of Neck Shaping)*, sc in side edge of row above, place stitch marker.

Rnd 2: Sc in each of next 2 sts, sc in each of next 8 chs of ear, sc in each of next 7 sts of ear, bend ear forward, from WS work sl st in last st before ear, hdc in next sc on neck, dc in each of next 6 sc, hdc in last sc before next ear, sc in each of next 8 chs of ear, sc in each of next 7 sts of ear, bend ear forward, from WS work sl st in last st before ear, sc in each of last 10 sc.

Rnd 3: Sc in first sc, sk sl st and hdc under ear, hdc in next dc, dc in each of next 4 dc, hdc in next dc, sk sl st under ear, sc in last 10 sc. *(17 sts)*

Rnd 4: Sk first sc, sc in next hdc, hdc in next dc, dc in each of next 2 dc, hdc in next dc, sc in next hdc, sc dec in next 2 sts, sc in each of next 6 sc, sc dec in next 2 sc. *(14 sts)*

Rnd 5: Sc in each of first 6 sts, sc dec in next 2 sts, sc in each of next 4 sts, sc dec in next 2 sts. *(12 sts)*

With fiberfill, stuff Head.

Rnds 6 & 7: Sc in each of next 12 sc.

Rnd 8: [Sc dec in next 2 sc] around until opening is closed. Fasten off.

Leg

Make 4.

Rnd 1: With size G hook and C, starting with foot, ch 2, 6 sc in 2nd ch from hook, do not join. *(6 sc)*

Rnds 2–5: Sc in each sc around. At the end of rnd 5, **change color** *(see Stitch Guide)* to E.

Rnd 6: Working with E, [2 sc in next sc, sc in next sc] 3 times. *(9 sc)*

Rnds 7–9: Working in back lps, sc in each st around. At the end of last rnd, sl st in next st, Leaving a 15-inch length, fasten off.

Rnd 10: Join B in first free lp on rnd 6 of Leg, sc in same st as beg sl st, *knot lp st in next st, sc in next st, rep from * over Leg, ending with sc in last st. Fasten off.

With fiberfill, stuff Leg lightly. Sew Leg to Body.

Tail

Row 1: With size G hook and C, ch 10, sc in 2nd ch from hook, sc in each of next 7 chs, 3 sc in last ch (tip), working on opposite side of foundation ch, sc in each of next 8 chs, turn. *(19 sc)*

Row 2: Ch 2, hdc in each of next 8 sc, sc in each of next 3 sc at tip, hdc in each of next 8 sc. Leaving 12-inch length, fasten off.

Matching sts, sew row 2 tog; sew Tail to back of Body.

Finishing

For eyes, sew 2 buttons to rnd 3 of Head, leaving 2 dc free between. To avoid choking hazard of young children, with light blue yarn, ch 2, 5 sc in 2nd ch from hook, leaving 5-inch length of yarn, **join** *(see Pattern Notes)* in beg sc. Sew crocheted eyes in place.

With tapestry needle and length of D, work **straight stitches** *(see illustration)* to cover tip of nose and end of each foot.

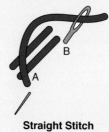

Straight Stitch

Tie pink satin ribbon in a bow around neck. ●

Baby Blocks Afghan & Pillow Set

Designs by Glenda Winkleman

Skill Level

■■■□ **INTERMEDIATE**

Finished Sizes
Afghan: 30½ x 38 inches
Pillow: 11 x 16 inches

Materials
- Red Heart Soft Baby Steps medium (worsted) weight yarn (solids: 5 oz/256 yds/142g per ball; prints: 4 oz/204 yds/113g per ball):
    25 oz # 9600 white *(A)*
    15 oz #9930 binky print *(F)*
    5 oz each # 9700 baby pink *(B)*, #9200 baby yellow *(C)*, #9800 baby blue *(D)* and #9620 baby green *(E)*
- Sizes H/8/5mm and I/9/5.5mm crochet hooks or size needed to obtain gauge
- Size J/10/6mm afghan crochet hook or size needed to obtain gauge
- Tapestry needle
- Fiberfill

Gauge
Afghan hook:, 16 sts = 4 inches; 15 rows = 4 inches;
Size H hook: 3 rnds = 3 inches

Pattern Notes
Weave in loose ends as work progresses.

Join with slip stitch as indicated unless otherwise stated.

Chain-3 at beginning of round counts as first double crochet unless otherwise stated.

Afghan
Block
Make 120.
Note: Working rnd 1, make 30 each B, C, D and E.

Rnd 1: With size H hook and indicated color, ch 5, **join** *(see Pattern Notes)* in first ch to form ring, **ch 3** *(see Pattern Notes)*, 2 dc in ring, ch 2, (3 dc in ring, ch 2) 3 times in ring, join in 3rd ch of beg ch-3. Fasten off. *(12 dc)*

Rnd 2: Join F in any corner ch-2 sp, ch 3, (dc, ch 2, 2 dc) in same corner ch-2 sp, sk next dc, 2 dc in next dc, sk next dc, [(2 dc, ch 2, 2 dc) in corner ch-2 sp, sk next dc, 2 dc in next dc, sk next dc] around, join in 3rd ch of beg ch-3. Fasten off. *(24 dc)*

Rnd 3: Join A in any corner ch-2 sp, ch 3, (2 dc, ch 2, 3 dc) in same corner ch-2 sp, [sk next 2 dc, 2 dc in sp between dc sts] twice,

sk next 2 dc, *(3 dc, ch 2, 3 dc) in next corner ch-2 sp, [sk next 2 dc, 2 dc in sp between dc sts] twice, sk next 2 dc, rep from * around, join in 3rd ch of beg ch-3. Fasten off.

Assembly

With size H hook and A, following placement chart, join blocks, working in **back lps** *(see Stitch Guide)* of sts of Rnd 3 matching sts, sc Blocks tog 10 by 12 blocks.

Border

Rnd 1: With size H hook, join A in top right-hand corner ch-2 sp, ch 3, 4 dc in same corner ch-2 sp, dc in each dc and each ch sp on each side of each joining seam around, work 5 dc in each corner ch-2 sp, join in 3rd ch of beg ch-3. Fasten off.

Rnd 2: Join F in top of beg ch-3 of previous rnd, ch 1, sc in each of first 2 dc, (ch 3, sl st) in last sc made, *sc in each of next 2 dc, (ch 3, sl st) in last sc made, rep from * around, join in beg sc. Fasten off.

Row 1

COLOR KEY
- Baby pink block
- Baby green block
- Baby yellow block
- Baby blue block

**Baby Blocks Afghan
Assembly Chart**

Pillow
Panel
Make 2.
With size J afghan hook and A, ch 49.

Row 1: Working right to left, insert hook in 2nd ch from hook, yo, draw through st, [insert hook in next ch, yo, draw through st] across, retaining all lps on hook *(49 lps)*, yo, draw yarn through 1 lp on hook, [yo, draw through 2 lps on hook] across until 1 lp remains on hook and counts as first st of next row.

Rows 2–30: Working from right to left, insert hook in 2nd vertical st from hook, yo, draw through st, [insert hook in next vertical st, yo, draw through st] across, retaining all lps on hook *(49 lps)*, yo, draw through 1 lp on hook, [yo, draw through 2 lps on hook] across until

1 lp remains on hook and counts as first st of next row.

Row 31: Sl st in each vertical st across. Fasten off.

Panel Border
Rnd 1: With right side of Panel facing, with size I hook, join A in top right-hand corner st, ch 1, sc in each of first 4 sts, **sc dec** *(see Stitch Guide)* in next 2 sts, *[sc in each of next 4 sts, sc dec in next 2 sts] across to next corner, ch 2, sc in each row end st across edge, rep from * around, ch 2, join in beg sc.

Rnd 2: Ch 1, sc in each sc around, work 3 sc in each corner ch-2 sp, join to beg sc.

Working on 2nd Panel, rep rnds 1 and 2 of Panel Border.

Assembly

Rnd 3: Place WS of Panels tog, working through both thickness and matching sts, ch 1, sc in each sc around 3 sides, working across 4th side through top Panel only, sc in each rem sc around, join in beg sc. Fasten off.

Rnd 4: Join B in beg sc, ch 1, (sc, ch 3) in each sc around, join in beg sc. Fasten off.

Rnd 5: Join E in first ch-3 sp, ch 1, (sc, ch 3) in each ch-3 sp around, join in beg sc. Fasten off.

Rnd 6: With C, rep rnd 5.

Rnd 7: With D, rep rnd 5.

Cross-Stitch

Following chart, cross-stitch design on pillow front. With fiberfill, stuff pillow. Sew opening closed. •

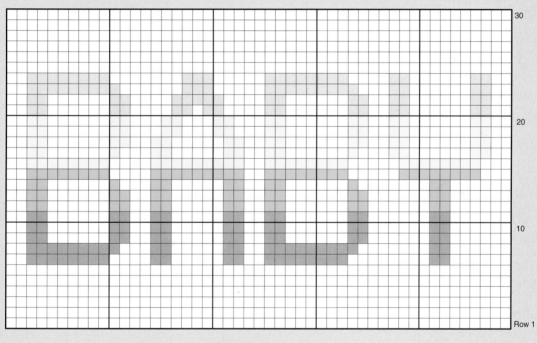

Baby Blocks Pillow

COLOR KEY
- Baby pink block
- Baby green block
- Baby yellow block
- Baby blue block

Merry Go 'Round the Block

Design by Sharon Ballsmith

Skill Level

◼◼◻◻ **EASY**

Finished Size

28 inches square

Materials

- Lion Brand Babysoft light (light worsted) weight yarn (5 oz/459 yds/141g per ball): 2 balls #170 pistachio
- Sizes G/6/4mm and H/8/5mm crochet hooks or size needed to obtain gauge
- Tapestry needle

Gauge

First 5 rnds = 4 inches square

Pattern Notes

Weave in loose ends as work progresses.

Join with slip stitch as indicated unless otherwise stated.

Chain-3 at beginning of round counts as first double crochet unless otherwise stated.

Special Stitch

Extra-long double crochet (x-long dc): Yo, insert hook in indicated st, yo, draw up lp, [yo, draw through 1 lp, yo, draw through 2 lps] twice.

Blanket
Body

Rnd 1: With size G hook, ch 4, 11 dc in 4th ch from hook, **join** (see Pattern Notes) in 4th ch of beg ch-4. (12 dc)

Rnd 2: Ch 3 (see Pattern Notes), 6 dc in same st as beg ch-3, [sk next 2 sts, 7 dc in next st] 3 times, join in 3rd ch of beg ch-3, turn. (28 dc)

Rnd 3: Ch 3, *(x-long dc—see Special Stitch, dc) in next dc, sk next 2 sts, 7 dc in next st, sk next 2 sts**, dc in next st, rep from * 3 times, ending last rep at **, join in 3rd ch of beg ch-3, turn. (40 sts)

Rnd 4: Ch 3, *(x-long dc, dc) in next st, sk next 2 sts, 7 dc in next st, sk next 2 sts, dc in next st, (x-long dc, dc) in next st, sk next st**, dc in next st, rep from * 3 times, ending last rep at **, join in 3rd ch of beg ch-3, turn. (52 sts)

Rnd 5: Ch 3, (x-long dc, dc) in next st, sk next st, *dc in next st, (x-long dc, dc) in next st, sk next 2 sts, 7 dc in next st, sk next 2 sts, [dc in next st, (x-long dc, dc) in next st, sk next st**] twice, rep from * 3 times, ending last rep at**, join in 3rd ch of beg ch-3, turn. (64 sts)

Rnd 6: Ch 3, (x-long dc, dc) in next st, sk next st, *dc in next st, (x-long dc, dc) in next st, sk next 2 sts, 7 dc in next st, sk next 2 sts**,

[dc in next st, (x-long dc, dc) in next st, sk next st] 3 times, rep from * 3 times, ending last rep at**, [dc in next st, (x-long dc, dc) in next st, sk next st] twice, join in 3rd ch of beg ch-3, turn. *(76 sts)*

Rnds 7–36: Continuing in the same manner as for rnd 6, each rnd will inc by 12 sts. As work progresses, always sk 1 st between each dc, (x-long dc, dc), and 2 sts before and after each 7-dc group at each corner, turn each rnd. Each rnd increases 1 group of dc, x-long dc and dc on each side for a total of 4-group increase, at the end of last rep a total of 436 sts. At the end of rnd 36, **do not fasten off.**

Buttonhole Edging

Rnd 37: *[Ch 5, sl st in next sp between groups *(pulling taut throughout rnd)*] rep across to corner 7 dc sts, ch 5, sk next 3 dc of corner, (sl st, ch 5, sl st) in next center dc of corner, ch 5, sk next 3 dc of corner, sl st in next sp between groups, rep from * around, join in same sp as beg ch-5, **do not turn.** *(148 ch-5 sps)*

Rnd 38: Ch 1, 5 sc in each ch-5 sp around, join in beg sc. Fasten off. *(740 sc)* •

Baby Squares

Design by Mickie Akins

Skill Level

▮▮▮▯ INTERMEDIATE

Finished Size

24½ x 28½ inches

Materials

- Bernat Baby Sport light (light worsted) weight yarn (12¼ oz/ 1256 yds/350g per ball):
  - 1 ball each #21718 sweet grass, #21615 baby yellow and #21005 baby white
- Size G/6/4mm crochet hook or size needed to obtain gauge
- Tapestry needle

Gauge

4 sc = 1 inch; 4 sc rows = 1 inch

Pattern Notes

Weave in loose ends as work progresses.

Join with slip stitch as indicated unless otherwise stated.

Blanket has six blocks across width.

Blanket
Body

Row 1: With baby white, ch 122, carrying sweet grass across and working over until needed, with baby white, sc in 2nd ch from hook, [**change color** (see Stitch Guide) to sweet grass and working over baby white, sc in each of next 19 chs, change color to baby white, working over sweet grass, sc in next sc] across, turn. (121 sc)

Note: Work over yarn color not in use throughout remainder of Blanket.

Row 2: Ch 1, with baby white, sc in next sc, [with sweet grass, sc in next sc, with baby white, sc in next 17 sc, with sweet grass, sc in next sc, with baby white, sc in next sc] across, turn.

Row 3: Ch 1, with baby white, sc in next sc, [with sweet grass, sc in next sc, with baby white, sc in next sc, with sweet grass, sc in each of next 15 sc, with baby white, sc in next sc, with sweet grass, sc in next sc, with baby white, sc in next sc] across, turn.

Row 4: Ch 1, [with baby white, sc in next sc, with sweet grass, sc in next sc] twice, *with baby white, sc in each of next 13 sc**, [with sweet grass, sc in next sc, with baby white, sc in next sc] 3 times, with sweet grass, sc in next sc, rep from * across, ending last rep at **, [with sweet grass, sc in next sc, with baby white, sc in next sc] twice, turn.

Row 5: Ch 1, [with baby white, sc in next sc, with sweet grass, sc in next sc] twice, with baby white, sc in next sc, *with sweet grass, sc in next 11 sc, with baby white, sc in next sc**, [with sweet grass, sc in next sc, with baby white, sc in next sc] 4 times, rep from * across, ending last rep at **, [with sweet grass, sc in next sc, with baby white, sc in next sc] twice, turn.

Row 6: Ch 1, [with baby white, sc in next sc, with sweet grass, sc in next sc] 3 times, *with baby white, sc in each of next 9 sc**, with sweet grass, sc in next sc, [with baby white, sc in next sc, with sweet grass, sc in next sc] 5 times, rep from * across, ending last rep at **, [with sweet grass, sc in next sc, with baby white, sc in next sc] 3 times, turn.

Row 7: Ch 1, with baby white, sc in next sc, [with sweet grass, sc in next sc, with baby white, sc in next sc] 3 times, *with sweet grass, sc in each of next 7 sc, with baby white, sc in next sc**, [with sweet grass, sc in next sc, with baby white, sc in next sc] 6 times, rep from * across, ending last rep at **, [with sweet grass, sc in next sc, with baby white, sc in next sc] 3 times, turn.

Row 8: Ch 1, [with baby white, sc in next sc, with sweet grass, sc in next sc] 4 times, *with baby white, sc in each of next 5 sc**, with sweet grass, sc in next sc, [with baby white, sc in next sc, with sweet grass, sc in next sc] 7 times, rep from * across, ending last rep at **, [with sweet grass, sc in next sc, with baby white, sc in next sc] 4 times, turn.

Row 9: Ch 1, with baby white, sc in next sc, [with sweet grass, sc in next sc, with baby white, sc in next sc] 4 times, *with sweet grass, sc in each of next 3 sc, with baby white, sc in next sc**, [with sweet grass, sc in next sc, with baby white, sc in next sc] 8 times, rep from * across, ending last rep at **, [with sweet grass, sc in next sc, with baby white, sc in next sc] 4 times, turn.

Row 10: Ch 1, with baby white, sc in next sc, [with sweet grass, sc in next sc, with baby white, sc in next sc] across, turn.

Row 11: Rep row 9.

Row 12: Rep row 8.

Row 13: Rep row 7.

Row 14: Rep row 6.

Row 15: Rep row 5.

Row 16: Rep row 4.

Row 17: Rep row 3.

Row 18: Rep row 2.

Row 19: Ch 1, with baby white, sc in next sc, [with sweet grass, sc in each of next 19 sc, with baby white, sc in next sc] across, turn. Fasten off baby white; draw up lp of baby yellow.

Note: Using chart as guide, sc in each st across. When repeating row 1, omit beg foundation ch following stitches on row 1 of chart and change color as indicated on chart.

Rows 20–38: With sweet grass (X) and baby yellow (O), rep rows 1–19 of chart.

Rows 39–57: With baby white (X) and baby yellow (O), rep rows 1–19 of chart.

Rows 58–76: With baby yellow (X) and sweet grass (O), rep rows 1–19 of chart.

Rows 77–95: With sweet grass (X) and baby white (O), rep rows 1–19 of chart.

Top Edging

Row 96: With baby yellow, ch 1, sc in first sc, [with sweet grass, sc in next sc, with baby yellow, sc in next sc] across, turn.

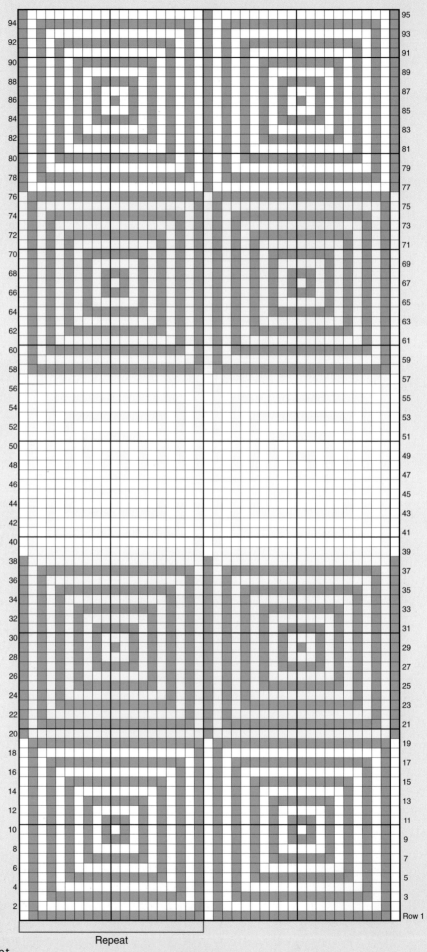

COLOR KEY
☐ Baby white
■ Sweet grass
☐ Baby yellow

Repeat

Blanket Chart

Rows 97–104: Ch 1, [sc in each baby yellow sc with baby yellow, sc in each sweet grass sc with sweet grass] across, turn. At the end of row 104, fasten off baby yellow.

Row 105: With sweet grass, ch 1, sc in each sc across. Fasten off.

Bottom Edging

Row 96: Working in opposite side of foundation ch, join baby yellow with sc in first ch, [with sweet grass, sc in next ch, with baby yellow, sc in next ch] across, turn.

Rows 97–104: Ch 1, [sc in each baby yellow sc with baby yellow, sc in each sweet grass sc with sweet grass] across, turn. At the end of row 104, fasten off baby yellow.

Row 105: With sweet grass, ch 1, sc in each sc across. Fasten off.

Side Border

Row 1: Working in side edge of Blanket rows, join baby yellow with sc in side edge of row 105 of Bottom Edging, sc in each row evenly sp to row 105 of Top Edging. Fasten off.

Row 2: Working in side edge of Blanket, join baby yellow with sc in side edge of row 105 of Top Edging, sc in each row evenly sp to row 105 of Bottom Edging. Fasten off. ●

Tiny Balloons

Designs by Mary Ann Sipes

Hat

Skill Level
■■■□ INTERMEDIATE

Finished Sizes
Instructions given for 12-inch circumference *(newborn–3 months)*; changes for 13-inch circumference *(3–6 months)* and 14-inch circumference *(6–12 months)* are in [ ].

Materials
- TLC Baby light (light worsted) weight yarn (6 oz/490 yds/170g per skein):
    1 oz #5881 powder blue
    ¼ oz #5011 white
- Size E/4/3.5mm, F/5/3.75mm and G/6/4mm crochet hook or size needed to obtain gauge
- Yarn needle
- 2-inch piece cardboard

Gauge
Size E hook: 4 dc and 2 dc rnds = ⅞ inch
Size F hook: 5 dc and 2 dc rnds = 1 inch
Size G hook: 4 dc and 2 dc rnds = 1⅛ inches

Pattern Notes
Weave in loose ends as work progresses.

Join with slip stitch as indicated unless otherwise stated.

Chain-3 at beginning of round counts as first double crochet unless otherwise stated.

Special Stitch
5-double crochet cluster (5-dc cl): [Yo, insert hook in indicated st, yo, draw up a lp, yo, draw through 2 lps on hook] 5 times in same st, yo, draw through all 6 lps on hook, ch 1 to lock. Push cl to RS of work.

Hat
Body
Rnd 1 (RS): With size E [F, G] hook and powder blue, loosely ch 60, using care not to twist, **join** *(see Pattern Notes)* in first ch, **ch 3** *(see Pattern Notes)*, dc in each rem ch around, join in 3rd ch of beg ch-3. *(60 dc)*

Rnd 2: Ch 3, dc in each of next 2 dc, **fpdc** *(see Stitch Guide)* around next dc, [dc in each of next 3 dc, fpdc around next dc] around, join in 3rd ch of beg ch-3. *(45 dc, 15 fpdc)*

Rnd 3: Ch 3, dc in each of next 2 dc, fpdc around next fpdc, [dc in each of next 3 dc, fpdc around next fpdc] around, join in 3rd ch of beg ch-3, turn.

Rnd 4: Ch 1, sc in first dc, **5-dc cl** *(see Special Stitch)* in next fpdc, [sc in each of next 3 dc, 5-dc cl in next fpdc] around, ending with sc in last 2 sts, join in beg sc, turn. *(45 sc, 15 5-dc cl)*

Rnd 5: Ch 1, sc in same st as beg ch-1, sc in each of next 2 sts, **sc dec** (*see Stitch Guide*) in next 2 sts, [sc in each of next 3 sts, sc dec in next 2 sts] around, join in beg sc. (*48 sc*)

Rnd 6: Ch 3, dc in each sc around, join in 3rd ch of beg ch-3.

Rnd 7: Ch 3, dc in each of next 4 dc, fpdc around next dc, [dc in each of next 5 dc, fpdc around next dc] around, join in 3rd ch of beg ch-3. (*40 dc, 8 fpdc*)

Rnd 8: Ch 3, dc in each of next 4 dc, fpdc around fpdc, [dc in each of next 5 dc, fpdc around fpdc] around, join in 3rd ch of beg ch-3, turn.

Rnd 9: Ch 1, sc in same dc as beg ch-1, 5-dc cl in next fpdc, [sc in each of next 5 dc, 5-dc cl in next dc] around, ending with sc in each rem 4 sc, join in beg sc, turn. (*40 sc, 8 5-dc cl*)

Rnd 10: Ch 1, sc in same sc as beg ch-1, sc in next sc, sc dec in next 2 sc, [sc in each of next 2 sc, sc dec in next 2 sc] around, join in beg sc. (*36 sc*)

Rnd 11: Ch 3, **dc dec** (*see Stitch Guide*) in next 2 sc, [dc in next dc, dc dec in next 2 sc] around, join in 3rd ch of beg ch-3. (*24 dc*)

Rnd 12: Ch 3, dc dec in next 2 dc, [dc in next dc, dc dec in next 2 dc] around, join in 3rd ch of beg ch-3. (*16 dc*)

Rnd 13: Ch 1, [sc dec in next 2 dc] 8 times, join in first sc. (*8 sc*)

Rnd 14: Ch 1, [sc dec in next 2 sc] 4 times, join in first sc. Fasten off. (*4 sc*)

Trim

Rnd 1 (RS): With top of Hat facing, join white in first ch of opposite side of foundation ch, ch 1, sc in same ch as beg ch-1, sc in each ch around, join in beg sc.

Rnd 2 (RS): Ch 1, reverse sc (*see Stitch Guide*) in each st around, join in beg sc. Fasten off.

Pompom

Cut 12-inch length of powder blue and set aside. Holding 1 strand each powder blue and white, wind around 2-inch piece of cardboard 40 times. Gently slip off cardboard and tie 12-inch strand tightly around center of strands, clip ends of strands, fluff and trim again as needed. Tie Pompom to top of Hat.

Bootie
Skill Level

■■■□ INTERMEDIATE

Finished Sizes

Instructions given for sole length 3¼ inches (*newborn–3 months*); changes for 3¾ inches (*3–6 months*) and 4¼ inches (*6–12 months*) are in [ ].

Materials

- TLC Baby light (light worsted) weight yarn (6 oz/490 yds/170g per skein):
    1 oz #5881 powder blue
    ¼ oz #5011 white
- Size E/4/3.5mm, F/5/3.75mm and G/6/4mm crochet hook or size needed to obtain gauge
- Yarn needle

Gauge

Size E hook: 4 dc and 2 dc rnds = ⅞ inch
Size F hook: 5 dc and 2 dc rnds = 1 inch
Size G hook: 4 dc and 2 dc rnds = 1⅛ inches

Pattern Notes

Weave in loose ends as work progresses.

Join with slip stitch as indicated unless otherwise stated.

Chain-3 at beginning of round counts as first double crochet unless otherwise stated.

Special Stitch

5-double crochet cluster (5-dc cl): [Yo, insert hook in indicated st, yo, draw up a lp, yo, draw through 2 lps on hook] 5 times in same st, yo, draw through all 6 lps on hook, ch 1 to lock. Push cl to RS of work.

Bootie
Make 2.

Sole

Rnd 1 (RS): With size E [F, G] hook and powder blue, loosely ch 11, 3 sc in 2nd ch from hook, sc in each of next 8 chs, 5 sc in last ch, working on opposite side of foundation ch, sc in each of next 8 chs, 2 sc in same ch as beg sc sts, **join** *(see Pattern Notes)* in **back lp** *(see Stitch Guide)* of first sc. *(26 sc)*

Rnd 2: Working in back lps, **ch 3** *(see Pattern Notes)*, dc in same st as beg ch-3, 2 dc in next st, dc in each of next 3 sts, sc in each of next 3 sts, dc in each of next 3 sts, [2 dc in next st] 5 times, dc in each of next 3 sts, sc in each of next 3 sts, dc in each of next 3 sts, 2 dc in next st, join in 3rd ch of ch-3, **do not fasten off**. *(34 sts)*

Sides

Rnd 1: Working in back lps, ch 3, dc in each st around, join in 3rd ch of beg ch-3. *(34 dc)*

Rnd 2: Ch 3, dc in next dc, **fpdc** *(see Stitch Guide)* in next dc, [dc in each of next 2 dc, fpdc around next dc] 10 times, dc in last dc, join in 3rd ch of beg ch-3. *(11 fpdc, 23 dc)*

Rnd 3: Ch 3, dc in next dc, fpdc around next fpdc, [dc in each of next 2 dc, fpdc around next fpdc] 3 times, [**dc dec** *(see Stitch Guide)* in next 2 dc, fpdc around next fpdc] 4 times, [dc in each of next 2 dc, fpdc around next fpdc] 3 times, dc in last dc, join in 3rd ch of beg ch-3. *(11 fpdc, 19 dc)*

Rnd 4: Ch 1, sc in same st as beg ch-1, sc in each of next 11 sts, [dc dec over next 2 sts] 3 times, sc in each of next 12 sts, join in first sc, **do not fasten off**. *(24 sc, 3 dc)*

Cuff

Rnd 1: Ch 4 *(counts as first dc, ch 1)*, [sk next st, dc in next st, ch 1] 13 times, join in 3rd ch of beg ch-4. *(14 ch-1 sps)*

Rnd 2: Ch 1, 2 sc in each ch-1 sp around, join in beg sc. *(28 sc)*

Rnd 3: Ch 3, dc in each of next 2 sts, fpdc around vertical post of next dc 2 rnds below, [dc in each of next 3 sts, fpdc around vertical post of next dc 2 rnds below] around, join in 3rd ch of beg ch-3. *(7 fpdc, 21 dc)*

Rnd 4: Ch 3, dc in each of next 2 dc, fpdc around next fpdc, [dc in each of next 3 dc, fpdc around next fpdc] 6 times, join in 3rd ch of beg ch-3, turn.

Rnd 5: Ch 1, sc in same st as beg ch-1, [5-dc cl in next fpdc, sc in each of next 3 dc] around, ending with sc in each of next 2 dc, join in beg sc. Fasten off. *(7 5-dc cl, 21 sc)*

Trim

Rnd 1 (RS): Join white in first sc of previous rnd, ch 1, sc in same st as beg ch-1, sc in each of next 2 sc, sc in ch-1 sp of next 5-dc cl, [sc in each of next 3 sc, sc in ch-1 sp of next 5-dc cl] around, join in beg sc. *(28 sc)*

Rnd 2: Ch 1, work reverse sc *(see Stitch Guide)* in each st around, join in beg sc. Fasten off.

Sole Trim

Rnd 1: With Sole facing, working in rem free lp of rnd 2 of Sole, join white, ch 1, sc in each st around, join in beg sc. *(34 sc)*

Rnd 2: Ch 1, work reverse sc *(see Stitch Guide)* in each st around, join in beg sc. Fasten off.

Tie

Make 2.
With white, ch 75, beg in 2nd ch from hook, sl st in **back bar of ch** *(see illustration)*, sl st in each ch across. Fasten off.

Back Bar of Chain

Starting at center front, weave tie through ch-1 sps of rnd 1 of Cuff. Tie ends in a bow at center front.

Blanket

Skill Level

■■■□ INTERMEDIATE

Finished Size

28 inches square

Materials

- TLC Baby light (light worsted) weight yarn (6 oz/490 yds/170g per skein):
  2 skeins #5881 powder blue
  1 oz #5011 white
- Size F/5/3.75mm crochet hook or size needed to obtain gauge
- Yarn needle

Gauge

2 dc rows = 1 inch; 4 dc = 1 inch; [1 sc row, 3 dc rows] twice, 1 sc row, 1 dc row = 4 inches

Pattern Notes

Weave in loose ends as work progresses.

Join with slip stitch as indicated unless otherwise stated.

Chain-3 at beginning of row or round counts as first double crochet unless otherwise stated.

Special Stitch

5-double crochet cluster (5-dc cl): [Yo, insert hook in indicated st, yo, draw up a lp, yo, draw through 2 lps on hook] 5 times in same st, yo, draw through all 6 lps on hook, ch 1 to lock. Push cl to RS of work.

Blanket
Body

Row 1 (RS): With powder blue, loosely ch 97, dc in 4th ch from hook, dc in each rem ch across, turn. *(95 dc)*

Row 2: Ch 3 *(see Pattern Notes)*, dc in each of next 6 dc, [**bpdc** *(see Stitch Guide)* around next dc, dc in each of next 7 dc] across, turn. *(84 dc, 11 bpdc)*

Row 3: Ch 3, dc in each of next 6 dc, [**fpdc** *(see Stitch Guide)* around bpdc, dc in each of next 7 dc] across, turn. *(84 dc, 11 fpdc)*

Row 4: Ch 1, sc in first dc, sc in each of next 6 dc, [**5-dc cl** *(see Special Stitch)* in next fpdc, sc in each of next 7 dc] across, turn. *(84 sc, 11 5-dc cl)*

Row 5: Ch 3, dc in each of next 6 sc, [dc in ch-1 sp of 5-dc cl, dc in each of next 7 sc] across, turn. *(95 dc)*

Row 6: Ch 3, dc in each of next 10 dc, bpdc around next dc, [dc in each of next 7 dc, bpdc around next dc] 9 times, dc in each of next 11 dc, turn. *(85 dc, 10 bpdc)*

Row 7: Ch 3, dc in each of next 10 dc, fpdc around next bpdc, [dc in each of next 7 dc, fpdc around next bpdc] 9 times, dc in each of next 11 dc, turn. *(85 dc, 10 fpdc)*

Row 8: Ch 1, sc in first dc, sc in each of next 10 dc, 5-dc cl in next fpdc, [sc in each of next 7 dc, 5-dc cl in next fpdc] 9 times, sc in each of next 11 dc, turn. *(85 sc, 10 5-dc cl)*

Row 9: Ch 3, dc in each of next 10 sc, dc in ch-1 sp of 5-dc cl, [dc in each of next 7 sc, dc in ch-1 sp of 5-dc cl] 9 times, dc in each of next 11 dc, turn. *(95 dc)*

Rows 10–57: [Rep rows 2–9 consecutively] 6 times.

Rows 58–61: [Rep rows 2–5 consecutively] once.

Row 62: Ch 3, dc in each dc across, turn, **do not fasten off.**

Border

Rnd 1 (RS): Ch 3, 4 dc in same st as beg ch-3 *(corner)*, dc in each of next 93 dc, 5 dc in last dc *(corner)*, working in ends of rows, dc in end of next row, [2 dc over end dc of each dc row, sk all sc rows *(93 dc)*, 5 dc in first ch on opposite side of foundation ch *(corner)*, dc in each of next 93 chs, 5 dc in next ch *(corner)*, working in ends of rows, dc in end of next row, [2 dc over end dc of each dc row, sk all sc rows *(93 dc)*, **join** *(see Pattern Notes)* in 3rd ch of beg ch-3.

Rnd 2 (RS): Ch 3, fpdc around next dc, *(dc in next dc, fpdc around post of same dc, dc in same dc), fpdc around next dc, [dc in next dc, fpdc around next dc] across to center corner dc, rep from * around, join in 3rd ch of beg ch-3. Fasten off.

Rnd 3 (RS): Join white in center corner fpdc, ch 1, [3 sc in center corner fpdc, sc in each st across to next center corner fpdc] around, join in beg sc.

Rnd 4 (RS): Ch 1, work reverse sc *(refer to Reverse Single Crochet diagram)* in each st around, join in beg sc. Fasten off. •

Rosebuds

Designs by Mary Ann Sipes

Hat
Skill Level
■■■□ INTERMEDIATE

Finished Sizes
Instructions given for 12-inch circumference *(newborn–3 months)*; changes for 13-inch circumference *(3–6 months)* and 14-inch circumference *(6–12 months)* are in [ ].

Materials
- TLC Baby light (light worsted) weight yarn (6 oz/490 yds/170g per skein):
    1¼ oz #5737 powder pink
    ¼ oz #5011 white
- Size E/4/3.5mm, F/5/3.75mm and G/6/4mm crochet hook or size needed to obtain gauge
- 2-inch piece of cardboard
- Yarn needle

Gauge
Size E hook: 4 sc and 4 sc rnds = ⅞ inch
Size F hook: 5 sc and 4 sc rnds = 1 inch
Size G hook: 4 sc and 4 sc rnds = 1⅛ inches

Pattern Notes
Weave in loose ends as work progresses.

Join with slip stitch as indicated unless otherwise stated.

Chain-3 at beginning of round counts as first double crochet unless otherwise stated.

Special Stitch
Popcorn (pc): Work 4 sc in indicated st, draw up lp, remove hook, insert hook in first sc of 4-sc group, pick up dropped lp and draw through st on hook.

Hat
Body
Rnd 1 (RS): With size E [F, G] hook and powder pink, loosely ch 60, using care not to twist ch, **join** *(see Pattern Notes)* in first ch, ch 1, sc in each ch around, join in beg sc. *(60 sc)*

Rnd 2: Ch 1, sc in each sc around, join in first sc.

Rnd 3: Working in **back lps** *(see Stitch Guide)*, ch 1, sc in same st as beg ch-1, sc in each st around, join in beg sc.

Rnd 4: Ch 1, sc in same sc as beg ch-1, sk next sc, dc in free lp 1 row below next sc, sc in next sc on this row, dc in same lp as previous dc 1 row below, sk next sc, [sc in next sc on this row, dc in free lp 1 row below next sc, sc in next sc on this row, dc in same lp as previous dc 1 row below, sk next sc] around, join in beg sc. *(60 sts)*

Rnd 5: Ch 1, [sc in next sc, ch 2, sk next dc, **pc** *(see Special Stitch)* in next sc, ch 2, sk next dc] around, join in beg sc. *(15 pc)*

Rnd 6: Ch 1, 2 sc in each ch-2 sp around, join in beg sc. *(60 sc)*

Rnd 7: Rep rnd 2.

Rnd 8: Rep rnd 3.

Rnd 9: Rep rnd 2.

Rnd 10: Working in back lps, ch 1, sc in same sc as beg ch-1, sc in each of next 2 sc, **sc dec** *(see Stitch Guide)* in next 2 sc, [sc in each of next 3 sc, sc dec in next 2 sc] around, join in beg sc. *(48 sc)*

Rnd 11: Rep rnd 4. *(48 sts)*

Rnd 12: Rep rnd 5. *(12 pc)*

Rnd 13: Rep rnd 6. *(48 sts)*

Rnd 14: Rep rnd 2.

Rnd 15: Rep rnd 3.

Rnd 16: Rep rnd 2.

Rnd 17: Working in back lps, ch 1, sc in same sc as beg ch-1, sc in next sc, sc dec in next 2 sc, [sc in each of next 2 sc, sc dec in next 2 sc] around, join in beg sc. *(36 sc)*

Rnd 18: Rep rnd 4. *(36 sts)*

Rnd 19: Rep rnd 5. *(9 pc)*

Rnd 20: Rep rnd 6.

Rnd 21: Rep rnd 2.

Rnd 22: Working in back lps, ch 1, sc in same sc as beg ch-1, sc dec in next 2 sc, [sc in next sc, sc dec in next 2 sc] around, join in beg sc. *(24 sc)*

Rnd 23: Rep rnd 2.

Rnd 24: Ch 1, sc in same sc as beg ch-1, sc dec in next 2 sc, [sc in next sc, sc dec in next 2 sc] around, join in beg sc. *(16 sc)*

Rnd 25: Ch 1, [sc dec in next 2 sc] 8 times, join in beg sc. *(8 sc)*

Rnd 26: Ch 1, [sc dec in next 2 sc] 4 times, join in beg sc. Fasten off. *(4 sc)*

Trim
Rnd 1 (RS): With top of Hat facing, join white in foundation ch, working loosely, ch 1, sc in same st as beg ch-1, sc in each ch around, join in beg sc. *(60 sc)*

Rnd 2: Ch 1, sc in same st as beg ch-1, ch 3, sk next 3 sc, [sc in next sc, ch 3, sk next 3 sc] around, join in beg sc. *(15 ch-3 sps)*

Rnd 3: Ch 1, [4 sc in next ch-3 sp, sl st in next sc] around, join in beg sc. Fasten off.

Pompom
Cut 12-inch length of powder pink and set aside. Holding 1 strand each powder pink and white, wind around 2-inch piece of cardboard 40 times. Gently slip off cardboard and tie 12-inch strand tightly around center of strands, clip ends of strands, fluff and trim again as needed. Tie Pompom to top of Hat.

Bootie
Skill Level
◼◼◼◻ **INTERMEDIATE**

Finished Sizes
Instruction given for sole length 3¼ inches *(newborn–3 months)*; changes for 3¾ inches *(3–6 months)* and 4¼ inches *(6–12 months)* are in [ ].

Materials
- TLC Baby light (light worsted) weight yarn (6 oz/490 yds/170g per skein):
    1 oz #5737 powder pink
    ¼ oz #5011 white
- Size E/4/3.5mm, F/5/3.75mm and G/6/4mm crochet hook or size needed to obtain gauge
- Yarn needle
- ¼-inch-wide white ribbon: 1 yd

Gauge
Size E hook: 4 dc and 2 dc rnds = ⅞ inch
Size F hook: 5 dc and 2 dc rnds = 1 inch
Size G hook: 4 dc and 2 dc rnds = 1⅛ inches

Pattern Notes
Weave in loose ends as work progresses.

Join with slip stitch as indicated unless otherwise stated.

Chain-3 at beginning of round counts as first double crochet unless otherwise stated.

Special Stitch
Popcorn (pc): Work 4 sc in indicated st, draw up lp, remove hook, insert hook in first sc of 4-sc group, pick up dropped lp and draw through st on hook.

Bootie
Make 2.

Sole
Rnd 1 (RS): With size E [F, G] hook and powder pink, loosely ch 11, 3 sc in 2nd ch from hook, sc in each of next 8 chs, 5 sc in last ch, working on opposite side of foundation ch, sc in each of next 8 chs, 2 sc in same ch as beg sc sts, **join** *(see Pattern Notes)* in back lp of first sc. *(26 sc)*

Rnd 2: Working in **back lps** *(see Stitch Guide)*, **ch 3** *(see Pattern Notes)*, dc in same st as beg ch-3, 2 dc in next st, dc in each of next 3 sts, sc in each of next 3 sts, dc in each of next 3 sts, [2 dc in next st] 5 times, dc in each of next 3 sts, sc in each of next 3 sts, dc in each of next 3 sts, 2 dc in next st, join in 3rd ch of ch-3, **do not fasten off.** *(34 sts)*

Sides
Rnd 1: Working in back lps, ch 1, sc in each of next 16 sts, 2 sc in next st, sc in each of next 2 sts, 2 sc in next st, sc in each of next 14 sts. *(36 dc)*

Rnd 2: Working in back lps, ch 1, sc in same st as beg ch-1, sc in each st around, join in beg sc.

Rnd 3: Ch 1, sc in same sc as beg ch-1, sk next sc, dc in free lp 1 row below next sc, sc in next sc on this row, dc in same lp as previous dc 1 row below, sk next sc, [sc in next sc on this row, dc in free lp 1 row below next sc, sc in next sc on this row, dc in same lp as previous dc 1 row below, sk next sc] around, join in beg sc.

Rnd 4: Ch 1, sc in same st as joining, ch 2, sk next dc, **pc** *(see Special Stitch)* in next st, [ch 2, sk next dc, sc in next sc, ch 2, sk next dc, pc in next sc] around, join in beg sc.

Rnd 5: Ch 1, 2 sc in each ch-2 sp around, join in beg sc. *(36 sc)*

Rnd 6: Ch 1, sc in same st as beg ch-1, sc in each of next 10 sc, dc in each of next 2 sc, **dc dec** *(see Stitch Guide)* in next 2 sc, ch 1, sk next 2 sts, dc dec in next 2 sc, ch 1, sk next 2 sts, dc dec in next 2 sts, dc in each of next 2 sc, sc in each rem 11 sts around, join in beg sc. *(31 sts)*

Rnd 7: Ch 1, sc in same st as beg ch-1, sc in each of next 11 sts, dc dec in next 2 sts, sk next ch-1 sp, pc in next dc dec, ch 1, sk next ch-1 sp, dc dec in next 2 sts, sc in each of next 12 sts, join in beg sc. *(27 sts)*

Cuff
Rnd 1: Ch 4 *(counts as first dc, ch 1)*, [sk next st, dc in next st, ch 1] 6 times, sk next pc, sk next dc dec, [dc in next st, ch 1, sk next st] 6 times, join in 3rd ch of beg ch-4. *(13 ch-1 sps)*

Rnd 2: Ch 1, 2 sc in each ch-1 sp around, join in beg sc. *(26 sc)*

Rnd 3: Ch 1, 2 sc in same st as beg ch-1, sc in each of next 11 sts, 2 sc in next st, sc in each of next 13 sts, join in beg sc. *(28 sc)*

Rnd 4: Working in back lps, ch 1, sc in same st as beg ch-1, sc in each st around, join in beg sc.

Rnd 5: Ch 1, sc in same sc as beg ch-1, sk next sc, dc in free lp 1 row below next sc, sc in next sc on this row, dc in same lp as previous dc 1 row below, sk next sc, [sc in next sc on this row, dc in free lp 1 row below next sc, sc in next sc on this row, dc in same lp as previous dc 1 row below, sk next sc] around, join in beg sc.

Rnd 6: Ch 1, sc in same st as joining, ch 2, sk next dc, pc in next st, [ch 2, sk next dc, sc in next sc, ch 2, sk next dc, pc in next sc] around, join in beg sc.

Rnd 7: Ch 1, [2 sc in next ch-2 sp, sc in next pc, 2 sc in next ch-2 sp, sl st in next sc] around, join in beg sc. Fasten off.

Trim
Rnd 1 (RS): Join white in first sc, [sc in each of next 5 sc, sl st in next sc] around. Fasten off.

Sole Trim
Rnd 1: With Sole facing, working in rem free lp of rnd 2 of Sole, join white, ch 1, sc in each st around, join in beg sc.

Rnd 2: Ch 1, [working in reverse sc *(see Stitch Guide)*, work from left to right, insert hook in next st from front to back, draw up lp on hook, yo, and draw through both lps on hook] around, join in beg sc. Fasten off.

Tie
Make 2.
Cut ribbon in half. Starting at center front, weave ribbon through ch-1 sps of rnd 1 of Cuff. Tie ends in a bow at center front.

Blanket

Skill Level
■■■□ INTERMEDIATE

Finished Size
27 inches square

Materials

- TLC Baby light (light worsted) weight yarn
  (6 oz/490 yds/170g per skein):
  2 skeins #5737 powder pink
  1¼ oz #5011 white
- Size F/5/3.75mm crochet hook or size
  needed to obtain gauge
- Yarn needle

Gauge
5 sc =1 inch; 4 sc rows = 1 inch

Pattern Notes
Weave in loose ends as work progresses.

Join with slip stitch as indicated unless
otherwise stated.

Chain-3 at beginning of row or round
counts as first double crochet unless
otherwise stated.

Special Stitch
Popcorn (pc): Work 4 sc in indicated st, draw
up lp, remove hook, insert hook in first sc
of 4-sc group, pick up dropped lp and draw
through st on hook.

Blanket
Body
Row 1 (RS): With powder pink, loosely ch 98,
sc in 2nd ch from hook, sc in each rem ch
across, turn. *(97 sc)*

Rows 2–4: Ch 1, sc in each sc across, turn.

Row 5: Ch 1, working in **back lps** *(see Stitch
Guide)*, sc in same st as beg ch-1, sc in each st
across, turn.

Row 6 (WS): Ch 1, sc in first sc, sk next sc, dc
in free lp on RS 1 row below next sc, sc in next
sc on this row, dc in same lp as previous dc
on RS 1 row below, sk next sc, [sc in next sc
on this row, dc in free lp on RS 1 row below
next sc, sc in next sc on this row, dc in same lp
as previous dc on RS 1 row below, sk next sc]
across, sc in last sc on this row, turn. *(97 sts)*

Row 7: Ch 1, sc in first sc, [ch 2, sk next dc,
pc *(see Special Stitch)* in next sc, ch 2, sk next
dc, sc in next sc] across, turn. *(24 pc)*

Row 8: Ch 1, 2 sc in each ch-2 sp across, sc in
last sc, turn. *(97 sc)*

Rows 9–12: Ch 1, sc in each sc across, turn.

Rows 13–124: [Rep rows 5–12 consecutively]
14 times. At the end of last rep, **do not
fasten off.**

Border
Rnd 1 (RS): Ch 1, (sc, ch 1, sc) in first sc, [ch 1,
sk next sc, sc in next sc] across to corner
(48 ch-1 sps between corners), (sc, ch 1, sc) in
last sc for corner, [ch 1, sk next 2 sc rows, sc in
next ending sc row] across to corner *(48 ch-1
sps)*, (sc, ch 1, sc) in corner ch of foundation
ch, [ch 1, sk next ch, sc in next ch] across

foundation ch *(48 ch-1 sps)*, (sc, ch 1, sc) in last ch of foundation ch, [ch 1, sk next 2 sc rows, sc in next ending sc row] across to corner *(48 ch-1 sps)*, join in beg sc. Fasten off.

Rnd 2: With RS facing, join white in upper right corner ch-1 sp, ch 1, *(sc, ch 1, sc) in corner ch-1 sp, ch 1, sk next sc, [sc in next ch-1 sp, ch 1, sk next sc] across to next corner ch-1 sp, rep from * around, join in beg sc.

Rnd 3: Ch 1, *3 sc in corner ch-1 sp, sc in each sc and each ch-1 sp across to next corner ch-1 sp, rep from * around, join in beg sc.

Rnd 4: Ch 1, sc in same sc as beg ch-1, ch 4, sk next sc, [sc in next sc, ch 4, sk next 3 sc] across to next corner, *ch 4, sk next sc, sc in center corner sc, ch 4, sk next sc, [sc in next sc, ch 4, sk next sc] across to next corner, rep from * around, join in beg sc.

Rnd 5: Ch 1, [5 sc in next ch-4 sp, sl st in next sc] around, join in beg sc.

Rnd 6: Sl st to center sc of 5-sc group, ch 1, sc in same sc as beg ch-1, ch 5, [sc in center sc of next 5-sc group, ch 5] around, join in beg sc.

Rnd 7: Ch 1, [5 sc in next ch-4 sp, sl st in next sc] around, join in beg sc. Fasten off. •

Shell & Popcorn Papoose Set

Designs by Frances Hughes

Skill Level

◼◼◻◻ EASY

Finished Size

Papoose: 19 inches long, 22-inch chest
Hat circumference: 16 inches

Materials

- Red Heart Moon & Stars medium (worsted) weight yarn (1¾ oz/ 110 yds/50g per skein):
    4 skeins #3624 limeade
- Size H/8/5mm crochet hook or size needed to obtain gauge
- Yarn needle

Gauge

3 dc rnds = 2 inches; 6 dc = 1½ inches; petal of (sc, ch 3, 3 dc) twice = 2 inches

Pattern Notes

Weave in loose ends as work progresses.

Join with slip stitch as indicated unless otherwise stated.

Chain-3 at beginning of row or round counts as first double crochet unless otherwise stated.

Special Stitches

Shell: (2 dc, ch 2, 2 dc) in indicated st or sp.

Beginning shell (beg shell): (ch 3, dc, ch 2, 2 dc) in indicated st or sp

Popcorn (pc): 4 dc in indicated st, draw up lp, remove hook, insert hook in first dc, pick up dropped lp, draw through st on hook.

Papoose & Hat
Papoose

Rnd 1: Beg at bottom, ch 4, **join** (see Pattern Notes) in first ch to form a ring, **ch 3** (see Pattern Notes), 11 dc in ring, join in 3rd ch of beg ch-3. *(12 dc)*

Rnd 2: Ch 3, dc in same st as beg ch-3, 2 dc in each dc around, join in 3rd ch of beg ch-3. *(24 dc)*

Rnd 3: Ch 3, dc in same st as beg ch-3, dc in next dc, [2 dc in next dc, dc in next dc] around, join in 3rd ch of beg ch-3. *(36 dc)*

Rnd 4: Ch 3, dc in same st as beg ch-3, dc in each of next 2 dc, [2 dc in next dc, dc in each of next 2 dc] around, join in 3rd ch of beg ch-3. *(48 dc)*

Rnd 5: Ch 3, dc in same dc as beg ch-3, dc in each of next 3 dc, [2 dc in next dc, dc in each of next 3 dc] around, join in 3rd ch of beg ch-3. *(60 dc)*

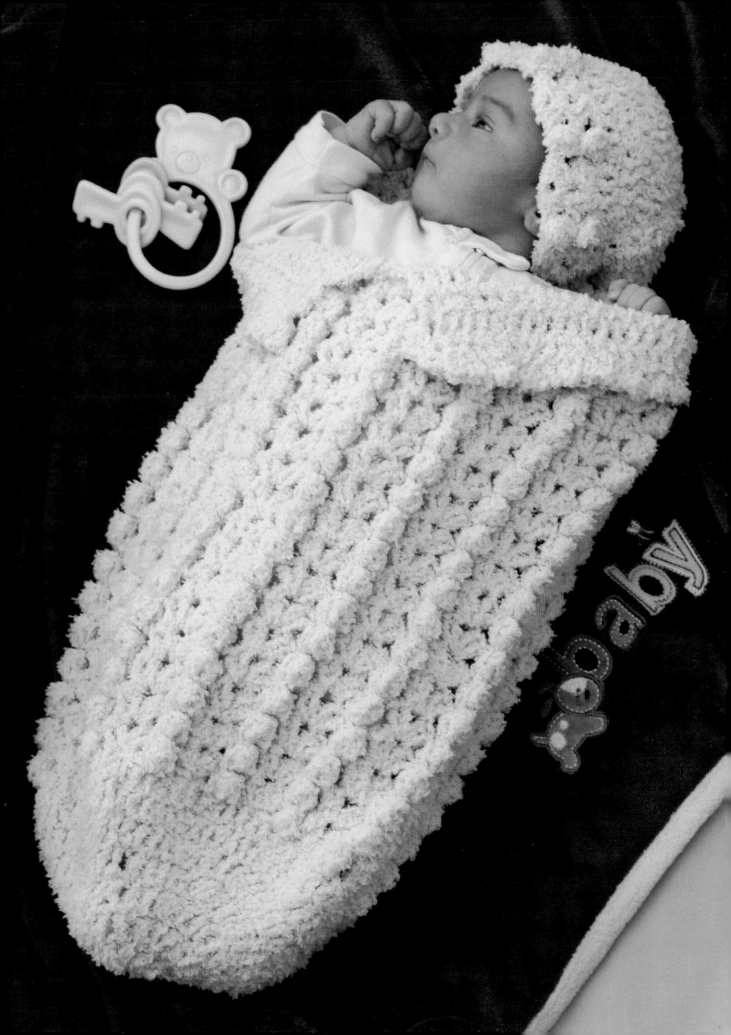

Rnd 8: Beg shell *(see Special Stitches)* in same dc as joining, sk next 2 dc, **pc** *(see Special Stitches)* in next dc, sk next 2 dc, [**shell** *(see Special Stitches)* in next dc, sk next 2 dc, pc in next dc, sk next 2 dc] around, join in 3rd ch of beg ch-3. *(13 shells, 13 pc)*

Rnds 9–24: Sl st into ch-2 sp, beg shell in same ch-2 sp, pc in top of next pc, [shell in ch-2 sp of next shell, pc in top of next pc] around, join in 3rd ch of beg ch-3.

Row 25: Now working in rows, sl st into ch-2 sp, ch 3, dc in each dc, dc in each pc and sk each ch-2 sp of each shell, ending with dc in same ch-2 sp as beg ch-3, turn, **do not join**.

Rows 26–29: Ch 3, dc in each dc across, turn.

Row 30: Ch 1, sc in same dc as beg ch-1, [ch 3, sc in next dc] across. Fasten off.

Hat

Rnds 1–4: Rep rnds 1–4 of Papoose. *(48 dc)*

Rnds 5–7: Ch 3, dc in each dc around, join in 3rd ch of beg ch-3. *(48 dc)*

Rnd 6: Ch 3, dc in same st as beg ch-3, dc in each of next 4 dc, [2 dc in next dc, dc in each of next 4 dc] around, join in 3rd ch of beg ch-3. *(72 dc)*

Rnd 7: Ch 3, dc in same st as beg ch-3, dc in each of next 11 dc, [2 dc in next dc, dc in each of next 11 dc] around, join in 3rd ch of beg ch-3. *(78 dc)*

Rnd 8: Beg shell in first dc, sk next 2 dc, pc in next dc, sk next 2 dc, [shell in next dc, sk next 2 dc, pc in next dc, sk next 2 dc] around, join in 3rd ch of beg ch-3. *(8 shells, 8 pc)*

Rnd 9: Sl st in ch-2 sp, beg shell in same ch-2 sp, pc in next pc, [shell in ch-2 sp of next shell, pc in next pc] around, join in 3rd ch of beg ch-3. Fasten off. ●

Shell Stitch Papoose & Hat

Designs by Sue Childress

Skill Level

■■□□ EASY

Finished Size

Papoose: 18½ inches long, 22-inch chest
Hat circumference: 16 inches

Materials

- Red Heart Moon & Stars medium (worsted) weight yarn (1¾ oz/ 110 yds/50g per skein):
    4 skeins #3805 blue frosting
- Size H/8/5mm crochet hook or size needed to obtain gauge
- Yarn needle

Gauge

3 dc rnds = 2 inches; 6 dc = 1½ inches; 2 shells = 2 inches

Pattern Notes

Weave in loose ends as work progresses.

Join with slip stitch as indicated unless otherwise stated.

Chain-3 at beginning of round counts as first double crochet unless otherwise stated.

Special Stitch

Shell: (Sc, ch 3, 3 dc) in indicated st or sp.

Papoose & Hat
Papoose

Rnd 1: Beg at bottom, ch 4, **join** *(see Pattern Notes)* in first ch to form a ring, **ch 3** *(see Pattern Notes)* 11 dc in ring, join in 3rd ch of beg ch-3. *(12 dc)*

Rnd 2: Ch 3, dc in same st as beg ch-3, 2 dc in each dc around, join in 3rd ch of beg ch-3. *(24 dc)*

Rnd 3: Ch 3, dc in same st as beg ch-3, 2 dc in next dc, dc in each of next 2 dc, [2 dc in each of next 2 dc, dc in each of next 2 dc] around, join in 3rd ch of beg ch-3. *(36 dc)*

Rnd 4: Ch 3, dc in same st as beg ch-3, 2 dc in next dc, dc in next dc, [2 dc in each of next 2 dc, dc in next dc] around, join in 3rd ch of beg ch-3. *(60 dc)*

Rnd 5: Ch 3, [dc in next dc, 2 dc in next dc] twice, [dc in each of next 2 dc, 2 dc in next dc, dc in next dc, 2 dc in next dc] 11 times, join in 3rd ch of beg ch-3. *(84 dc)*

Rnd 6: Ch 1, **shell** *(see Special Stitch)* in same dc as beg ch-1, sk next 3 dc, [shell in next dc, sk next 3 dc] around, join in beg sc. *(21 shells)*

Rnds 7–28: Sl st into ch-3 sp, ch 1, shell in same ch-3 sp, shell in each ch-3 sp around, join in beg sc.

Row 29: Now working in rows, sl st into ch-3 sp, ch 1, shell in same ch-3 sp, shell in each ch-3 sp across, turn, **do not join**. *(21 shells)*

Rows 30–32: Sl st into ch-3 sp, ch 1, shell in same ch-3 sp as beg ch-1, shell in each ch-3 sp across, turn.

At the end of row 32, fasten off.

Hat

Rnds 1–3: Rep rnds 1–3 of Papoose. *(36 dc)*

Rnd 4: Ch 3, dc in next dc, 2 dc in next dc, [dc in each of next 2 dc, 2 dc in next dc] 11 times, join in 3rd ch of beg ch-3. *(48 dc)*

Rnd 5: Ch 1, shell in same dc as beg ch-1, sk next 3 dc, [shell in next dc, sk next 3 dc] around, join in beg sc. *(12 shells)*

Rnds 6–9: Sl st into ch-3 sp, ch 1, shell in same ch-3 sp, shell in each ch-3 sp around, join in beg sc.

At the end of rnd 9, fasten off. ●

baby gifts

Baby's First Book

Design by Glenda Winkleman

Skill Level

◼◼◼▭ INTERMEDIATE

Finished Size

8½ inches wide x 9 inches tall x 2 inches thick

Materials

- Red Heart Super Saver medium (worsted) weight yarn (solids: 7 oz/364 yds/198g; flecks: 5 oz/260 yds/141g per skein):
    16 oz #311 white
    ½ oz each #324 bright yellow, #672 spring green, #885 delft blue, #319 cherry red, #312 black, #722 pretty 'n pink, #4334 buff fleck, #254 pumpkin and #360 café
- Size I/9/5.5mm afghan crochet hook or size needed to obtain gauge
- Size H/8/5mm crochet hook
- Yarn needle

Gauge

Size I hook: 17 sts = 4 inches; 14 rows = 4 inches

Pattern Notes

Weave in loose ends as work progresses.

Join with slip stitch as indicated unless otherwise stated.

Book

Block

Make 8.

Row 1: With size I hook and white, ch 32, working right to left, insert hook in 2nd ch from hook, yo, draw up lp, [insert hook in next ch, yo, draw up lp] across, retaining all lps on hook (*32 lps*), now working left to right, yo, draw through first lp on hook, [yo, draw through 2 lps on hook] across until 1 lp remains on hook and counts as first lp of next row.

Rows 2–29: Working right to left, insert hook in 2nd vertical st from hook, yo, draw lp through, [insert hook in next vertical st, yo, draw lp through] across, retaining all lps on hook (*32 lps*), now working left to right, yo, draw through first lp on hook, [yo, draw through 2 lps on hook] across until 1 lp remains on hook and counts as first lp of next row.

Row 30: Sl st in each vertical st across. Fasten off.

Cross-Stitch

Following charts on pages 130–137, cross-stitch designs on each Block.

Block Assembly

Rnd 1: With size H hook, holding 2 Blocks with WS facing and working through both thicknesses, insert hook in top right corner and draw up lp of white, ch 1, [sc in each st across to next corner, ch 1 to turn corner] around, **join** (*see Pattern Notes*) in beg sc. Fasten off.

Book Assembly

With yarn needle and white, working down left side of page and working in **back lps** (*see Stitch Guide*) of sc sts on first page and through **front lps** (*see Stitch Guide*) of sc on 2nd page, whipstitch first page to 2nd page; on 2nd page to 3rd page, work rem back lp of 2nd and front lp of 3rd page and back lp of 3rd page to front lp of 4th page.

Book Edging

Rnd 1: With RS of Book facing and size H hook, join bright yellow in top right corner sc of front cover, ch 1, sc in each sc across front cover, 2 sc in spine of Book, sc in each

sc across top of last page to next corner ch-1 sp (leaving inside pages unworked), work 2 sc in corner ch-1 sp, sc in each sc down side of last page to next corner ch-1 sp, 2 sc in corner ch-1 sp, sc in each sc across bottom of last page, 2 sc in Book spine, sc in each sc across bottom of front cover to next corner ch-1 sp, 2 sc in corner ch-1 sp, sc in each sc across side of front cover, ending with 2 sc in corner ch-1 sp at top corner, join in beg sc. Fasten off. •

COLOR KEY
- ☐ Bright yellow
- ☐ Spring green
- ☐ Delft blue
- ■ Cherry red
- ■ Black
- ■ Pretty n' pink
- ☐ Buff fleck
- ■ Pumpkin
- ■ Café

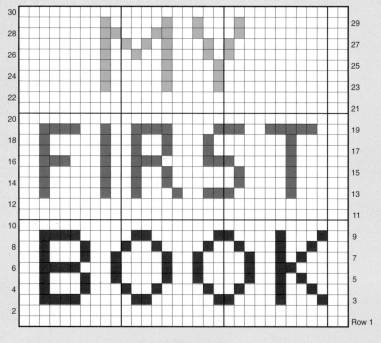

Baby's First Book

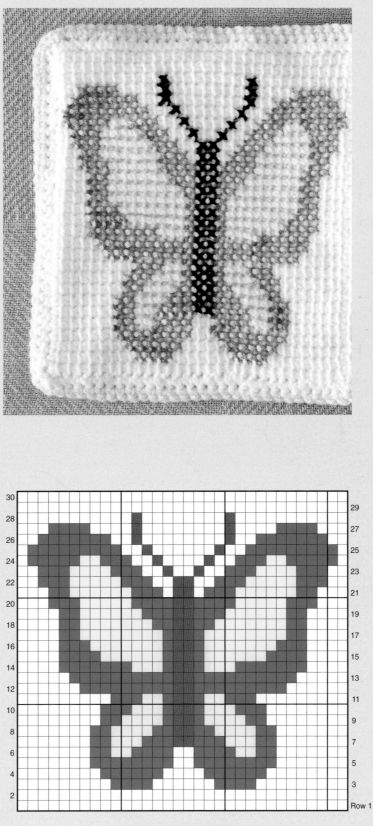

Baby's First Book

COLOR KEY
- Bright yellow
- Spring green
- Delft blue
- Cherry red
- Black
- Pretty n' pink
- Buff fleck
- Pumpkin
- Café

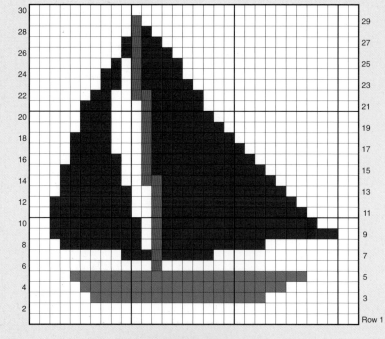

Baby's First Book

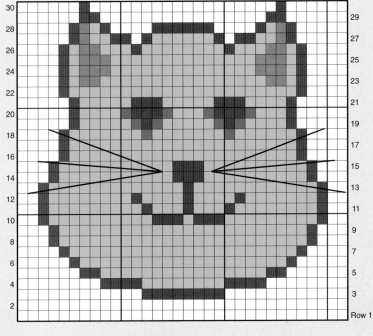

Baby's First Book

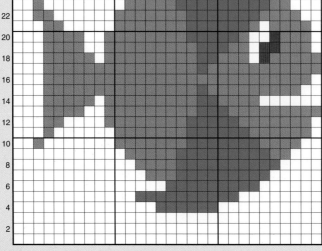

COLOR KEY
- ☐ Bright yellow
- ☐ Spring green
- ☐ Delft blue
- ■ Cherry red
- ■ Black
- ■ Pretty n' pink
- ☐ Buff fleck
- ■ Pumpkin
- ■ Café

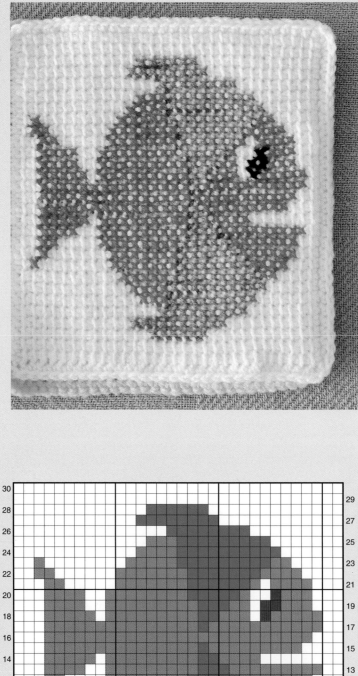

Baby's First Book

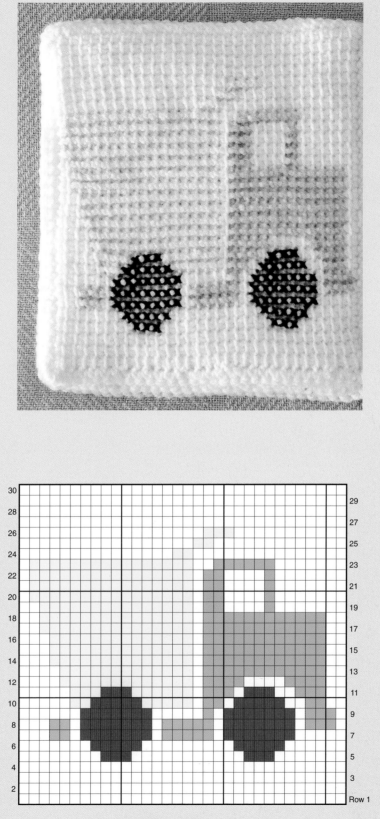

Baby's First Book

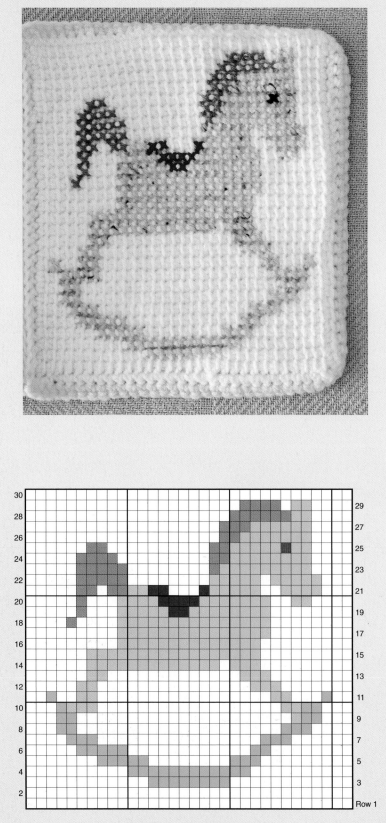

COLOR KEY
- ☐ Bright yellow
- ☐ Spring green
- ☐ Delft blue
- ■ Cherry red
- ■ Black
- ☐ Pretty n' pink
- ☐ Buff fleck
- ☐ Pumpkin
- ■ Café

Baby's First Book

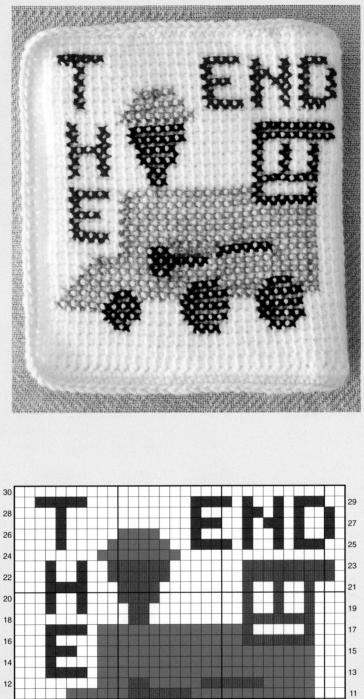

Baby's First Book

Toy Cat

Design by Michele Wilcox

Skill Level
■■□□ EASY

Finished Size
8 inches tall

Materials
- Plymouth Yarn Jeannee Worsted medium (worsted) weight yarn (110 yds/50g per ball):
    2 balls #17 light yellow
    1 ball #21 light blue
- Size F/5/3.75mm crochet hook or size needed to obtain gauge
- Tapestry needle
- 2 yds brown pearl cotton
- Fiberfill
- Stitch marker

Gauge
8 sts = 1½ inches; 8 rnds = 1½ inches

Pattern Notes
Weave in loose ends as work progresses.

Do not join rounds unless otherwise stated, use stitch marker to mark rounds.

Cat
Head

Rnd 1: Starting at top of Head with light yellow, ch 6, sc in 2nd ch from hook, sc in each of next 3 chs, 3 sc in last ch, working on opposite side of foundation ch, sc in each of next 3 chs, 2 sc in same ch as first sc, place stitch marker to mark rnds. *(12 sc)*

Rnd 2: 2 sc in first sc, sc in each of next 3 sc, 2 sc in each of next 3 sc, sc in each of next 3 sc, 2 sc in each of next 2 sc. *(18 sc)*

Rnd 3: [Sc in each of next 2 sc, 2 sc in next sc] around. *(24 sc)*

Rnd 4: Sc in each sc around.

Rnd 5: [Sc in each of next 3 sc, 2 sc in next sc] around. *(30 sc)*

Rnd 6: [Sc in each of next 4 sc, 2 sc in next sc] around. *(36 sc)*

Rnds 7 & 8: Rep rnd 4.

Rnd 9: [Sc in each of next 5 sc, 2 sc in next sc] around. *(42 sc)*

Rnds 10–17: Rep rnd 4.

Rnd 18: [Sc dec *(see Stitch Guide)* in next 2 sc] 4 times, sc in each of next 5 sc, [sc dec in next 2 sc] 8 times, sc in each of next 5 sc, [sc dec in next 2 sc] 4 times. *(26 sc)*

Rnd 19: [Sc dec in next 2 sc] twice, sc in each of next 5 sc, [sc dec in next 2 sc] 4 times, sc in each of next 5 sc, [sc dec in next 2 sc] twice. *(18 sc)*

Rnd 20: Rep rnd 4.

Body
Rnd 21: [Sc in each of next 2 sc, 2 sc in next sc] around. *(24 sc)*

Rnds 22–26: Rep rnd 4.

Rnd 27: Sc in each of next 6 sc, 2 sc in each of next 6 sc *(hind end)*, sc in each of next 12 sc. *(30 sc)*

Rnds 28–32: Rep rnd 4.

Rnd 33: [Sc in each of next 3 sc, sc dec in next 2 sc] around. *(24 sc)*

Rnd 34: [Sc in each of next 2 sc, sc dec in next 2 sc] around. *(18 sc)*

Stuff Head and Body with fiberfill.

Rnd 35: [Sc in next sc, sc dec in next 2 sc] around. *(12 sc)*

Rnd 36: [Sc dec in next 2 sc] around, sl st in next st. Leaving 6-inch length, fasten off. *(6 sc)*

Weave rem length through sts, draw opening closed, knot to secure. Fasten off.

Ear
Make 2.
Rnd 1: With light yellow, ch 2, 6 sc in 2nd ch from hook, place stitch marker to mark rnds. *(6 sc)*

Rnd 2: 2 sc in first sc, sc in each of next 5 sc. *(7 sc)*

Rnd 3: Sc in each of next 2 sc, 2 sc in next sc, sc in each of next 4 sc. *(8 sc)*

Rnd 4: Sc in each of next 4 sc, 2 sc in next sc, sc in each of next 3 sc. *(9 sc)*

Rnd 5: 2 sc in next sc, sc in each of next 8 sc. *(10 sc)*

Rnd 6: Sc in each of next 2 sc, 2 sc in next sc, sc in each of next 7 sc. Fasten off. *(11 sc)*

Stuff Ears lightly with fiberfill and sew in place.

Snout
Rnd 1: With light yellow, ch 6, sc in 2nd ch from hook, sc in each of next 3 chs, 3 sc in last ch, working on opposite side of foundation ch, sc in each of next 3 chs, 2 sc in same ch as first sc, place stitch marker to mark rnds. *(12 sc)*

Rnd 2: 2 sc in first sc, sc in each of next 3 sc, 2 sc in each of next 3 sc, sc in each of next 3 sc, 2 sc in each of next 2 sc. *(18 sc)*

Rnd 3: Sc in each sc around.

Sew to front of face, stuffing lightly.

Facial Features
With brown pearl cotton, embroider nose with **satin stitch** *(see illustration)*, **straight stitches** *(see illustration)* for mouth and whiskers and satin-stitch eyes.

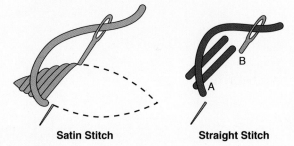

Satin Stitch   **Straight Stitch**

Arm
Make 2.
Rnd 1: With light yellow, ch 6, sc in 2nd ch from hook, sc in each of next 3 chs, 3 sc in last ch, working on opposite side of foundation ch, sc in each of next 3 chs, 2 sc in same ch as first sc, place stitch marker to mark rnds. *(12 sc)*

Rnds 2–9: Sc in each sc around. At the end of rnd 9, fasten off.

Stuff Arm with fiberfill. Form paws by sewing through all thicknesses at hand end 3 rnds up and going over tip of hand, draw sts tightly twice to shape 3 paws.

Leg
Make 2.
Rnd 1: Rep rnd 1 of Arm. *(12 sc)*

Rnd 2: 2 sc in first sc, sc in each of next 3 sc, 2 sc in each of next 3 sc, sc in each of next 3 sc, 2 sc in each of next 2 sc. *(18 sc)*

Rnd 3: Sc in each sc around.

Rnds 4 & 5: Rep rnd 3.

Rnd 6: [Sc in next sc, sc dec in next 2 sc] around. *(12 sc)*

Rnds 7–10: Rep rnd 3.

At the end of rnd 10, fasten off.

Stuff Leg with fiberfill. Form paws by sewing through all thicknesses at foot end 3 rnds up and going over tip of foot, draw sts tightly twice to shape 3 paws.

Tail

Rnd 1: With light yellow, ch 2, 6 sc in 2nd ch from hook. *(6 sc)*

Rnd 2: [Sc in next sc, 2 sc in next sc] around. *(9 sc)*

Rnds 3–21: Sc in each sc around, stuffing with fiberfill as work progresses. At the end of last rep, fasten off. Sew opening flat across, sew Tail in place.

Sweater
Turtleneck
Make 2.
Row 1: With light blue, ch 7, sc in 2nd ch from hook, sc in each rem ch across, turn. *(6 sc)*

Rows 2–14: Ch 1, working in **back lp** *(see Stitch Guide)*, sc in each st across, turn. At the end of row 14, **do not fasten off.**

Sweater Body
Row 1: Ch 1, working in ends of rows, sc in end of each of next 14 rows, turn. *(18 sc)*

Row 2: Ch 1, 2 sc in each of next 2 sc, sc in each of next 10 sc, 2 sc in each of next 2 sc, turn. *(18 sc)*

Row 3: Ch 1, sc in each sc across, turn.

Row 4: Sl st in each of next 2 sc, ch 1, sc in each of next 14 sc, leaving rem 2 sc unworked, turn. *(14 sc)*

Rows 5–10: Rep row 3. At the end of row 10, fasten off.

Sew ends of row tog from bottom edge up 4 rows, sew ends of turtleneck and through row 3 on each side of Sweater Body. Place Sweater on Cat and turn turtleneck down. ●

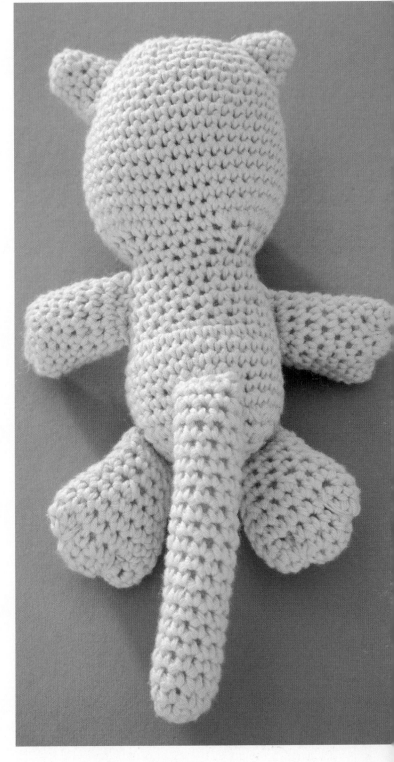

Toy Dog

Design by Michele Wilcox

Skill Level

■■□□ EASY

Finished Size

8 inches tall

Materials

- Plymouth Yarn Jeannee Worsted medium (worsted) weight yarn (110 yds/50g per ball):
    2 balls #5 brown
    1 ball #16 light green
- Size F/5/3.75mm crochet hook or size needed to obtain gauge
- Tapestry needle
- 2 yds black pearl cotton
- 18 inches red pearl cotton
- Fiberfill
- Stitch marker

Gauge

8 sts = 1½ inches; 8 rnds = 1½ inches

Pattern Notes

Weave in loose ends as work progresses.

Do not join rounds unless otherwise stated, use stitch marker to mark rounds.

Dog
Head

Rnd 1: Starting at top of Head with brown, ch 6, sc in 2nd ch from hook, sc in each of next 3 chs, 3 sc in last ch, working on opposite side of foundation ch, sc in each of next 3 chs, 2 sc in same ch as first sc, place stitch marker to mark rnds. *(12 sc)*

Rnd 2: 2 sc in first sc, sc in each of next 3 sc, 2 sc in each of next 3 sc, sc in each of next 3 sc, 2 sc in each of next 2 sc. *(18 sc)*

Rnd 3: [Sc in each of next 2 sc, 2 sc in next sc] around. *(24 sc)*

Rnd 4: Sc in each sc around.

Rnd 5: [Sc in each of next 3 sc, 2 sc in next sc] around. *(30 sc)*

Rnd 6: [Sc in each of next 4 sc, 2 sc in next sc] around. *(36 sc)*

Rnds 7 & 8: Rep rnd 4.

Rnd 9: [Sc in each of next 5 sc, 2 sc in next sc] around. *(42 sc)*

Rnds 10–17: Rep rnd 4.

Rnd 18: [**Sc dec** *(see Stitch Guide)* in next 2 sc] 4 times, sc in each of next 5 sc, [sc dec in next 2 sc] 8 times, sc in each of next 5 sc, [sc dec in next 2 sc] 4 times. *(26 sc)*

Rnd 19: [Sc dec in next 2 sc] twice, sc in each of next 5 sc, [sc dec in next 2 sc] 4 times, sc in each of next 5 sc, [sc dec in next 2 sc] twice. *(18 sc)*

Rnd 20: Rep rnd 4.

Body

Rnd 21: [Sc in each of next 2 sc, 2 sc in next sc] around. *(24 sc)*

Rnds 22–26: Rep rnd 4.

Rnd 27: Sc in each of next 6 sc, 2 sc in each of next 6 sc *(hind end)*, sc in each of next 12 sc. *(30 sc)*

Rnds 28–32: Rep rnd 4.

Rnd 33: [Sc in each of next 3 sc, sc dec in next 2 sc] around. *(24 sc)*

Rnd 34: [Sc in each of next 2 sc, sc dec in next 2 sc] around. *(18 sc)*

Stuff Head and Body with fiberfill.

Rnd 35: [Sc in next sc, sc dec in next 2 sc] around. *(12 sc)*

Rnd 36: [Sc dec in next 2 sc] around, sl st in next st. Leaving 6-inch length, fasten off. *(6 sc)*

Weave rem length through sts, draw opening closed, knot to secure. Fasten off.

Arm

Make 2.

Rnd 1: With brown, ch 6, sc in 2nd ch from hook, sc in each of next 3 chs, 3 sc in last ch, working on opposite side of foundation ch, sc in each of next 3 chs, 2 sc in same ch as first sc, place stitch marker to mark rnds. *(12 sc)*

Rnds 2–9: Sc in each sc around. At the end of rnd 9, fasten off.

Stuff Arm with fiberfill. Form paws by sewing through all thicknesses at hand end 3 rnds up and going over tip of hand, draw sts tightly twice to shape 3 paws.

Leg

Make 2.

Rnd 1: Rep rnd 1 of Arm. *(12 sc)*

Rnd 2: 2 sc in first sc, sc in each of next 3 sc, 2 sc in each of next 3 sc, sc in each of next 3 sc, 2 sc in each of next 2 sc. *(18 sc)*

Rnd 3: Sc in each sc around.

Rnds 4 & 5: Rep rnd 3.

Rnd 6: [Sc in next sc, sc dec in next 2 sc] around. *(12 sc)*

Rnds 7–10: Rep rnd 3.

At the end of rnd 10, fasten off.

Stuff Leg with fiberfill. Form paws by sewing through all thicknesses at foot end 3 rnds up and going over tip of foot, draw sts tightly twice to shape 3 paws.

Ear

Make 2.

Rnd 1: With brown, ch 2, 6 sc in 2nd ch from hook, place stitch marker to mark rnds. *(6 sc)*

Rnd 2: 2 sc in each sc around. *(12 sc)*

Rnd 3: Sc in each sc around.

Rnd 4: [Sc in next sc, 2 sc in next sc] around. *(18 sc)*

Rnds 5–8: Rep rnd 3.

Rnd 9: [Sc in next sc, sc dec in next 2 sc] around. *(12 sc)*

Rnds 10–14: Rep rnd 3. Do not stuff Ears, fold rnd 14 flat across and sew in place.

Snout

Rnd 1: With brown, ch 2, 6 sc in 2nd ch from hook, place stitch marker to mark rnds. *(6 sc)*

Rnd 2: [Sc in each of next 2 sc, 2 sc in next sc] around. *(8 sc)*

Rnd 3: Sc in each sc around.

Rnd 4: [Sc in each of next 3 sc, 2 sc in next sc] around. *(10 sc)*

Rnd 5: [Sc in each of next 4 sc, 2 sc in next sc] around. *(12 sc)*

Rnd 6: [Sc in each of next 5 sc, 2 sc in next sc] around. *(14 sc)*

Rnd 7: [Sc in each of next 6 sc, 2 sc in next sc] around. *(16 sc)*

Rnd 8: [Sc in each of next 7 sc, 2 sc in next sc] around. *(18 sc)*

Rnd 9: [2 sc in next sc] 6 times, sc in each of next 12 sc. *(24 sc)*

Rnd 10: Sc in each sc around.

Stuff Snout with fiberfill and sew to front of face.

Mouth Bottom

Rnd 1: With brown, ch 2, 6 sc in 2nd ch from hook, place stitch marker to mark rnds. *(6 sc)*

Rnd 2: [Sc in next sc, 2 sc in next sc] around. *(9 sc)*

Rnds 3 & 4: Sc in each sc around. At the end of rnd 4, fasten off.

Sew centered under Snout.

Facial Features

With red pearl cotton, embroider tongue in **satin stitch** *(see illustration)*. With black pearl cotton, sew nose and eyes with **straight stitches** *(see illustration)*.

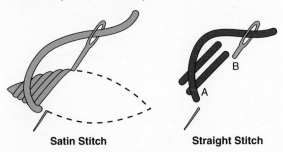

Satin Stitch   **Straight Stitch**

Tail

Rnd 1: With brown, ch 2, 6 sc in 2nd ch from hook. *(6 sc)*

Rnd 2: [Sc in each of next 2 sc, 2 sc in next sc] around. *(8 sc)*

Rnd 3: Sc in each sc around.

Rnd 4: [Sc in each of next 3 sc, 2 sc in next sc] around. *(10 sc)*

Rnds 5–9: Sc in each sc around, stuffing with fiberfill as work progresses. At the end of last rep, fasten off. Sew opening flat across, sew Tail in place.

Sweater
Turtleneck

Make 2.
Row 1: With light green, ch 7, sc in 2nd ch from hook, sc in each rem ch across, turn. *(6 sc)*

Rows 2–14: Ch 1, working in **back lp** *(see Stitch Guide)*, sc in each st across, turn. At the end of row 14, **do not fasten off**.

Sweater Body

Row 1: Ch 1, working in ends of rows, sc in end of each of next 14 rows, turn. *(18 sc)*

Row 2: Ch 1, 2 sc in each of next 2 sc, sc in each of next 10 sc, 2 sc in each of next 2 sc, turn. *(18 sc)*

Row 3: Ch 1, sc in each sc across, turn.

Row 4: Sl st in each of next 2 sc, ch 1, sc in each of next 14 sc, leaving rem 2 sc unworked, turn. *(14 sc)*

Rows 5–10: Rep row 3. At the end of row 10, fasten off.

Sew ends of row tog from bottom edge up 4 rows, sew ends of turtleneck and through row 3 on each side of Sweater Body. Place Sweater on Dog and turn turtleneck down. •

Baby Cloche

Design by Nancy Nehring

Skill Level
■■□□ EASY

Finished Sizes
Instructions given fit newborn (*5 x 16 inches circumference*); changes for size 9 months (*5½ x 18 inches circumference*) and toddler (*6 x 20 inches circumference*) are in [ ].

Materials
- Red Heart Zoomy super bulky (super chunky) weight yarn (3½ oz/83 yds/100g per ball):
   1 ball each #8275 candy pink (*MC*)
- Red Heart Soft Yarn medium (worsted) weight yarn (5 oz/256 yds/140g per ball):
   1 ball #4600 white
- Size M/13/9mm crochet hook or size needed to obtain gauge
- Size H/8/5mm crochet hook
- Yarn needle

Gauge
Size M hook: 12 sts = 4 inches; 18 rows = 4 inches

Pattern Note
Weave in loose ends as work progresses.

Cloche
Body

Row 1: With size H hook and white, ch 6, **change color** (*see Stitch Guide*) to MC and size M hook, ch 13 [15, 17], beg in 2nd ch from hook, sl st in **back lp** (*see Stitch Guide*) of each of next 12 [14, 16] sts, change color to white and size H hook, sl st in back lp of each of next 6 sts, turn. (*18 [20, 22] sts*)

Note: *Always use size M hook with MC and H hook with white yarn.*

Row 2: Ch 1, sl st in back lp of each of next 6 sts, change color to MC, sl st in back lp of each of next 10 [12, 14] sts, leaving last 2 sts unworked, turn. (*16 [18, 20] sts*)

Row 3: Ch 1, sl st in back lp of each of next 10 [12, 14] sts, change color to white, sl st in back lp of each of next 6 sts, turn.

Row 4: Ch 1, sl st in back lp of each of next 6 sts, change color to MC, sl st in back lp of each of next 8 [10, 12] sts, leaving last 2 sts unworked, turn. (*14 [16, 18] sts*)

Row 5: Ch 1, sl st in back lp of each of next 8 [10, 12] sts, change color to white, sl st in back lp of each of next 6 sts, turn.

Row 6: Ch 1, sl st in back lp of each of next 6 sts, change color to MC, sl st in back lp of each of next 6 [8, 10] sts, leaving last 2 sts unworked, turn. (*12 [14, 16] sts*)

Row 7: Ch 1, sl st in back lp of each of next 6 [8, 10] sts, change color to white, sl st in back lp of each of next 6 sts, turn.

Row 8: Ch 1, sl st in back lp of each of next 6 sts, change color to MC, sl st in back lp of each of next 12 [14, 16] sts (*6 [8, 10] sts of row 7, next 2 sts of row 5, next 2 sts of row 3 and next 2 sts of row 1*), turn. (*12 [14, 16] sts*)

Row 9: Ch 1, sl st in back lp of each of next 12 [14, 16] sts, change color to white, sl st in back lps of each of next 6 sts, turn.

Rows 10–72 [10–80, 10–88]: [Rep rows 2–9 consecutively] 8 [9, 10] times, ending last rep with row 8.

Row 73 [81, 89]: Holding last row to opposite side of foundation ch, sl st in each st across. Fasten off.

With a length of MC, weave through sts at center top of Cloche, draw opening closed, knot to secure. Fasten off. •

Pretty Edgings

Designs by Lisa Naskrent

Skill Level

■■□□ EASY

Finished Size

Edgings measure 1¼-1½ inches-wide

Materials

- Plymouth Yarn Jeannee Worsted medium (worsted) weight yarn (110 yds/50g per ball): 2 balls #16 light green and #27 shrimp 1 ball #32 yellow
- Size F/5/3.75mm crochet hook or size needed to obtain gauge
- Tapestry needle
- 27½-inch flannel blanket: 3
- ⅝-inch-wide white satin ribbon: 5 yds

Gauge

17 sts = 4 inches; 20 rows = 4 inches

Pattern Notes

Weave in loose ends as work progresses.

Join with slip stitch as indicated unless otherwise stated.

Special Stitches

Scallop: [Dc, (ch 1, dc) 5 times] in indicated st.

Large Scallop (lg scallop): [Dc, (ch 1, dc) 6 times] in indicated st.

Popcorn (pc): 5 sc in indicated st, draw up lp, remove hook, insert hook in first sc of 5-sc group, pick up dropped lp and draw through st on hook, ch 1 to lock.

Cluster (cl): Yo, insert hook in indicated st, yo, draw up lp, yo, draw through 2 lps on hook, [yo, insert hook in same st, yo, draw up lp, yo, draw through 2 lps on hook] 3 times, yo, draw through all 5 lps on hook.

Picot: Ch 3, sl st in 3rd ch from hook.

Fabric Preparation

Any fabric with an edging (*pre-sewn*) to work crochet sc sts into will work. If fabric is plain, hand sew **blanket stitch** (*see illustration*) with yarn needle, with sts ¼ inch from edge and ¼ to ½ inch apart.

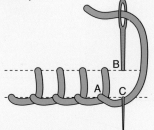

Blanket Stitch

Edgings
Yellow Edging

Rnd 1: Ch 1, sc around evenly, ending with multiple of 12 sts, **join** (*see Pattern Notes*) in beg sc.

Note: *When working rnd 2 around corners, work **lg scallop** (see Special Stitches) as needed to keep work flat.*

Rnd 2: Ch 1, sc in each of next 7 sc, sk next 2 sc, **scallop** *(see Special Stitches)* in next sc, sk next 2 sc, [sc in each of next 7 sc, sk next 2 sc, scallop in next sc, sk next 2 sc] around, join in beg sc.

Rnd 3: Sl st in next sc, ch 1, sc in same sc, sc in next sc, *pc *(see Special Stitches)* in next sc, sc in each of next 2 sc, sk next sc, (sc, ch 3, sc) in each ch-1 sp of next scallop, leaving dc sts of scallop unworked, sk next sc**, sc in each of next 2 sc, rep from * around, ending last rep at **, join in first sc. Fasten off.

Shrimp Edging

Rnd 1: Ch 1, sc around evenly, ending with multiple of 4 sts, **join** *(see Pattern Notes)* in beg sc.

Rnd 2: Ch 4 *(counts as first dc, ch 1)*, sk next st, [dc in next st, ch 1, sk next st] around, working (dc, ch 1, dc) around corners as needed to keep corners flat, join in 3rd ch of beg ch-4.

Rnd 3: Ch 1 *(draw up ch-1 to height of dc)*, leaving ch-3 st unworked, sk next ch-1 sp, **fpdc** *(see Stitch Guide)* around next dc, ch 2, working in front of fpdc just made, fpdc around post of unworked ch-3, sk next ch-1 sp, *sk next dc and next ch-1 sp, fpdc around next dc, ch 2, working in front of fpdc just made, fpdc around sk dc, sk next ch-1 sp, rep from * around, working ch 3 instead of ch 2 as needed in corners to keep work flat, join in top of first fpdc.

Rnd 4: Ch 1, 5 sc in each ch-2 sp or ch-3 sp around, join in beg sc. Fasten off.

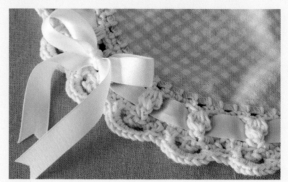

Green Edging

Rnd 1: Ch 1, sc around evenly, ending with multiple of 6 sts, **join** *(see Pattern Notes)* in beg sc.

Rnd 2: Ch 1, sc in same st as beg ch-1, ch 4, sk next 2 sts, **cl** *(see Special Stitches)* in next st, ch 4, sk next 2 sts, *sc in next st, ch 4, sk next 2 sts, cl in next st, ch 4, sk next 2 sts, rep from * around, join in first sc.

Rnd 3: Sl st in first ch-4 sp, ch 1, 4 sc in same ch sp, **picot** *(see Special Stitches)*, sk next cl, 4 sc in next ch-4 sp, *sk next sc, 4 sc in next ch-4 sp, picot, sk next cl, 4 sc in next ch-4 sp, rep from * around, join in beg sc.

Rnd 4: Sl st in next sc, ch 1, sc in same sc, sc in next sc, ch 5, sk next sc, picot and sc, sc in each of next 2 sc, ch 1, sk next 2 sc, *sc in each of next 2 sc, ch 5, sk next sc, picot and sc, sc in each of next 2 sc, ch 1, sk next 2 sc, rep from * around, join in beg sc.

Rnd 5: Sl st in next ch-5 sp, ch 1, 9 sc in same ch-5 sp, ch 2, [9 sc in next ch-5 sp, ch 2] around, working ch 3 instead of ch 2 at corners to keep work flat, join in beg sc. Fasten off.

Cut ribbon into 4 equal lengths of 45 inches.

Weave each length across each edge of rnd 3 by weaving under cl sts and over sc sts. After all lengths are woven, tie each corner lengths in a bow. ●

Baby Headbands

Designs by Frances Hughes

Skill Level
■■□□ EASY

Finished Sizes
Head circumference: Preemie 12–15 inches, baby 14–16 inches and toddler 16–18 inches

Finished Garment Sizes
Yellow Headband: 11–15 inches
Pink headband: 14–16 inches
White headband: 15–20 inches

Materials
- Cascade Fixation fine (sport) weight elastic yarn (100 yds/50g per ball): 1 ball each #8176 white, #1430 yellow and #3077 pink
- Size B/1/2.25mm crochet hook or size needed to obtain gauge
- Tapestry needle
- Sewing needle & thread
- Floral button
- 1½-inch silk flower & pearls ornament: 6

Gauge
5 dc = 1 inch; 3 dc rows = 1 inch

Pattern Notes
Weave in loose ends as work progresses.

Join with slip stitch as indicated unless otherwise stated.

Headbands are adjustable to length desired.

Chain-3 at beginning of row counts as first double crochet unless otherwise stated.

Special Stitches
Shell: 5 dc in indicated st.

Picot: Ch 3, sl st in first ch of ch-3.

Headbands

Yellow Headband
Row 1: With yellow, ch 8, dc in 4th ch from hook, dc in each rem ch across, turn. *(6 dc)*

Rows 2–38: Ch 3 *(see Pattern Notes)*, dc in each of next 5 dc, turn.

Row 39: Holding row 38 to opposite side of foundation ch, sl st in each st across. Fasten off.

Upper Bow Loops

Row 1: With yellow, ch 8, dc in 4th ch from hook, dc in each rem ch across, turn. *(6 dc)*

Rows 2–21: Ch 3, dc in each of next 5 dc, turn.

Row 22: Holding row 21 to opposite side of foundation ch, sl st in each st across. Fasten off.

Lower Bow Tails

Row 1: With yellow, ch 8, dc in 4th ch from hook, dc in each rem ch across, turn. *(6 dc)*

Rows 2–17: Ch 3, dc in each of next 5 dc, turn. At the end of row 17, fasten off.

Bow Band

Row 1: With yellow, ch 5, sc in 2nd ch from hook, sc in each rem ch across, turn. *(4 sc)*

Rows 2–15: Ch 1, sc in each sc across, turn. At the end of row 15, fasten off.

Finishing

With joining seams at center, place Upper Bow Loops on top of Lower Bow Tails. Wrap Bow Band around center of Bow sections and stitch in place. Stitch completed Bow over seam of Headband.

Pink Headband

Row 1: With pink, ch 6, dc in 4th ch from hook, dc in each rem ch across, turn. *(4 dc)*

Rows 2–36: Ch 3, dc in each of next 3 dc, turn.

Rnd 37: Now working in rnds, ch 1, working in side edge of rows, *sc in side edge of row 36, **picot** *(see Special Stitches)* in side edge of same row, [**shell** *(see Special Stitches)* in next row, (sc, picot) in next row] across edge*, holding row 36 to opposite side of foundation ch and working through both thicknesses, sl st across, ch 1, matching sc, picots and shells to opposite edge, rep between * once, **join** *(see Pattern Notes)* in first st. Fasten off.

Flower

Rnd 1: With pink, ch 4, join in first ch to form ring, ch 3, 11 dc in ring, join in 3rd ch of beg ch-3. *(12 dc)*

Rnd 2: Ch 3, dc in same st as beg ch-3, 2 dc in each dc around, join in 3rd ch of beg ch-3. *(24 dc)*

Rnd 3: Ch 1, (sc, 2 dc, sc) in same dc as beg ch-1, sl st in next sc, [(sc, 2 dc, sc) in next dc, sl st in next dc] around, join in beg sc. Fasten off.

Finishing

Stitch Flower over joining seam of Headband. Sew floral button to center of Flower.

White Headband

Row 1: With white, ch 77, dc in 4th ch from hook, dc in each rem ch across, turn. *(75 dc)*

Row 2: Ch 1, sc in first dc, [ch 3, sk next dc, sc in next dc] across, turn.

Rnd 3: Now working in rnds, holding ends of rows tog, sl st across ends of rows, working across opposite side of foundation ch, ch 1, sc in first ch, [ch 3, sk next ch, sc in next ch] across, **join** *(see Pattern Notes)* in first ch. Fasten off.

Finishing

Sew 6 silk pearl flowers evenly sp around Headband. •

Mary Jane Slippers

Design by Frances Hughes

Skill Level

■■□□ EASY

Finished Sizes

Instructions given fit infant's size 0–3 months and size 6–9 months.

Finished Garment Measurements

Sole: 3½ inches long *(size 0–3 months)*, [4½ inches long *(size 6–9 months)*]

Materials

- Schachenmayr Catania light (light worsted) crochet cotton (137 yds/ 50g per ball): 50 [75] yds desired color
- Size E/4/3.5mm crochet hook or size needed to obtain gauge
- Tapestry needle
- 12mm shank buttons: 2 per set
- Stitch marker

Gauge

5 sc = 1 inch

Pattern Notes

Weave in loose ends as work progresses.

Join with slip stitch as indicated unless otherwise stated.

Chain-2 at beginning of round counts as first half double crochet unless otherwise stated.

Slippers

Slippers Size 0–3 Months

Make 2.

Sole

Rnd 1: Ch 12, 2 hdc in 3rd ch from hook, hdc in next ch, sc in each of next 5 chs, hdc in next ch, 2 dc in next ch, 5 dc in last ch *(toe)*,

working on opposite side of foundation ch, 2 dc in next ch, hdc in next ch, sc in each of next 5 chs, hdc in next ch, 2 hdc in same ch as beg 2-hdc, **join** *(see Pattern Notes)* in top of beg ch. *(28 sts)*

Rnd 2: Ch 2 *(see Pattern Notes)*, hdc in same st as beg ch-2, hdc in next st, 2 hdc in next st, hdc in each of next 7 sts, 2 hdc in next st, 2 dc in each of next 7 sts, 2 hdc in next st, hdc in each of next 7 sts, 2 hdc in next st, hdc in next st, join in 2nd ch of beg ch-2. *(40 sts)*

Rnds 3 & 4: Ch 2, hdc in each st around, join in 2nd ch of beg ch-2. *(40 hdc)*

Rnd 5: Ch 2, hdc in each of next 14 sts, [**dc dec** *(see Stitch Guide)* in next 2 sts] 6 times, hdc in each of next 13 sts, join in 2nd ch of beg ch-2. *(34 sts)*

Rnd 6: Ch 1, sc in same st as beg ch-1, **sc dec** *(see Stitch Guide)* in next 2 sts, sc in each of next 11 sts, [dc dec in next 2 sts] 4 times, sc in each of next 10 sts, sc dec in next 2 sts, join in beg sc. Fasten off. *(28 sts)*

Strap

Row 1: Join yarn in 7th st from center back, ch 1, sc in same st as beg ch-1, sc in next st, turn.

Rows 2–8: Ch 1, sc in each of next 2 sc, turn.

Row 9: Ch 1, sc in first sc, ch 3 *(buttonhole)*, sc in 2nd sc. Fasten off.

On 2nd Slipper, beg Strap on opposite edge of Slipper.

Trim

Join yarn with sc in first st behind Strap, **reverse sc** *(see Stitch Guide)* in each st around to opposite edge of Strap. Fasten off.

Finishing

Sew button opposite buttonhole of Strap.

Slippers Size 6–9 Months
Make 2.

Sole

Rnd 1: Ch 16, 2 hdc in 3rd ch from hook, hdc in next ch, sc in each of next 9 chs, hdc in next ch, 2 hdc in next ch, 5 hdc in last ch *(toe)*, working on opposite side of foundation ch, 2 hdc in next ch, hdc in next ch, sc in each of next 9 chs, hdc in next ch, 2 hdc in same ch as beg 2-hdc, **join** *(see Pattern Notes)* in top of beg ch. *(36 sts)*

Rnd 2: Ch 2, hdc in same st as beg ch-2, hdc in next st, 2 hdc in next st, hdc in each of next 11 sts, 2 hdc in next st, dc in next st, [2 dc in next st, dc in next st] 3 times, 2 hdc in next st, hdc in each of next 11 sts, 2 hdc in next st, hdc in next st, join in 2nd ch of beg ch-2. *(44 sts)*

Rnds 3–5: Ch 3 *(counts as first dc)*, dc in each st around, join in 3rd ch of beg ch-3. *(44 dc)*

Rnd 6: Ch 2, hdc in each of next 15 sts, [**dc dec** *(see Stitch Guide)* in next 2 sts] 7 times, hdc in each of next 14 sts, join in 2nd ch of beg ch-2. *(37 sts)*

Rnd 7: Ch 1, sc in first st, **sc dec** *(see Stitch Guide)* in next 2 sts, sc in each of next 10 sts, [dc dec in next 2 sts] 6 times, sc in each of next 10 sts, sc dec in next 2 sts, join in beg sc. Fasten off. *(29 sts)*

Strap

Row 1: Join yarn in 9th st from center back, ch 1, sc in same st as beg ch-1, sc in next st, turn.

Rows 2–10: Ch 1, sc in each of next 2 sc, turn.

Row 11: Ch 1, sc in first sc, ch 3 *(buttonhole)*, sc in 2nd sc. Fasten off.

On 2nd Slipper, beg Strap on opposite edge of Slipper.

Trim

Join yarn with sc in first st behind Strap, **reverse sc** *(see illustration)* in each st around to opposite edge of Strap. Fasten off.

Finishing

Sew button opposite buttonhole of Strap. •

Embellished Slipper

Design by Sue Childress

Skill Level
■■□□ EASY

Finished Sizes
Instructions given fit infant's size 0–3 months; changes for 6–9 months are in [ ].

Finished Garment Measurements
Sole: 3½ inches long *(size 0–3 months)*, [4½ inches long *(size 6–9 months)*]

Materials
• Schachenmayr Catania light (light worsted) crochet cotton (137 yds/ 50g per ball):
   75 [100] yds desired color
• Size E/4/3.5mm crochet hook or size needed to obtain gauge
• Tapestry needle
• Embellishments as desired
• Stitch marker

Gauge
5 sc = 1 inch

Pattern Notes
Weave in loose ends as work progresses.

Join with slip stitch as indicated unless otherwise stated.

Chain-2 at beginning of row or round counts as first half double crochet unless otherwise stated.

Special Stitch
Back post single crochet (bpsc): Yo, insert hook back to front to back again around vertical post of indicated st, yo, draw up a lp, yo, draw through 2 lps on hook.

Slippers
Make 2.

***Note**: All slippers are the same pattern. We've tried to show different colors and different types of embellishment.*

Sole
Rnd 1: Ch 13 [17], 2 hdc in 3rd ch from hook, hdc in each of next 2 chs, sc in each of next 7 [11] chs, 6 hdc in last ch *(toe)*, working on opposite side of foundation ch, sc in each of next 7 [11] chs, hdc in each of next 2 chs, 2 hdc in same ch as beg 2-hdc, **join** *(see Pattern Notes)* in top of beg ch. *(29 [37] sts)*

Rnd 5: Ch 1, sc in each st around, join in beg sc.

Rnd 6: Fold Slipper in half lengthwise and place stitch marker in center st of toe, ch 1, sc in each st to within 6 sc of marked st, **dc dec** (see Stitch Guide) in next 2 sts, sc in each rem st, join in beg sc. (34 [42] sts)

Rnd 7: Fold Slipper in half lengthwise and place stitch marker in center st of toe, ch 1, sc to within 6 sts of marked st, [dc dec in next 2 sts] 6 times, sc in each rem st around, join in beg sc. (28 [36] sts)

Rnd 8: Fold Slipper in half lengthwise and place stitch marker in center st of toe, ch 2, hdc to within 4 sts of marked st, [dc dec in next 2 sts] 4 times, hdc in each rem st, join in 2nd ch of beg ch-2. (24 [32] sts)

Size 6–9 Months Only

Rnd 9: Fold Slipper in half lengthwise and place stitch marker in center st of toe, ch 2 hdc to within 6 sts of marked st, [dc dec in next 2 sts] 6 times, hdc in each rem st, join in 2nd ch of beg ch-2. [26 sts]

Both Sizes
Cuff

Row 9 [10]: Now working in rows, fold Slipper in half lengthwise and place stitch marker in center st of toe, sl st loosely to marked st at center front of toe, do not work marked st, turn, ch 2, hdc in each st to center front, turn. (23 [25] hdc)

Rows 10–12 [11–13]: Ch 2, hdc in each st across, turn.

Rnd 13 [14]: Now working in rnds, ch 1, sc in each hdc, at front opening, [2 sc over side edge of next row] 4 times, sc in marked st, [2 sc over side edge of next row] 4 times, join in beg sc. Fasten off.

For Cuff, fold down rows 10–13 [11–14].

Embellish center front of each Slipper. •

Rnd 2: Ch 2 (see Pattern Notes), hdc in same st as beg ch-2, hdc in each of next 2 sts, sc in each of next 9 [13] sts, [2 hdc in next hdc, hdc in next hdc] 3 times, sc in each of next 9 [13] sts, 2 hdc in next st, hdc in next st, join in 2nd ch of beg ch-2. (34 [42] sts)

Rnd 3: Ch 2, 2 hdc in next st, hdc in each of next 11 [15] sts, hdc in each of next 2 sts, [2 hdc in next st, hdc in next st] 3 times, 2 hdc in next st, hdc in each of next 11 [15] sts, 2 hdc in next st, join in 2nd ch of beg ch-2. (40 [48] hdc)

Sides

Rnd 4: Ch 1, **bpsc** (see Special Stitch) around each hdc around, join in 2nd ch of beg ch-2. (40 [48] sts)

Sock Trims

Designs by Norma Gale

Skill Level

■■■□ INTERMEDIATE

Finished Sizes

Instructions fit infant's size 6–24 months; changes for 24–36 months and toddler's size 3–5 are in [ ].

Materials

- J. & P. Coats Royale Classic Crochet size 10 crochet cotton (white: 400 yds; solids: 350 yds per ball):
    - 20 yds #201 white
    - 5 yds each #480 delft and #661 frosty green
- Size 9/1.25mm and 10/1.15mm steel crochet hooks or size needed to obtain gauge
- Tapestry needle
- 2 pairs of bobby socks

Gauge

Size 10 hook: 10 sc = 1 inch

Pattern Notes

Weave in loose ends as work progresses.

Join with slip stitch as indicated unless otherwise stated.

Sock Trims

Sock Trim No. 1

Make 2.

Rnd 1: Unroll cuff of sock; working on WS of sock with size 9 hook and white, place **slip knot** (see illustration) on hook, push hook through top edge of sock, yo, draw through sock, yo draw through 2 lps on hook, work 39 [43, 47] sc around top edge, **join** (see Pattern Notes) in first sc. (40 [44, 48] sc)

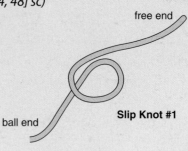

free end

ball end

Slip Knot #1

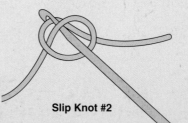

Slip Knot #2

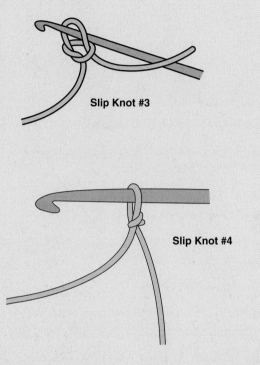

Slip Knot #3

Slip Knot #4

Rnd 2: With size 10 hook, working in **front lps** *(see Stitch Guide)*, ch 1, sc in same sc as beg ch-1, ch 3, sk next sc, [sc in next sc, ch 3, sk next sc] around, join in first sc. *(20 [22, 24] ch-3 sps)*

Rnd 3: Sl st in next ch-3 sp, ch 4 *(counts as first dc, ch 1)*, (dc, ch 1) 3 times in same ch-3 sp, sc in next ch-3 sp, ch 1, [(dc, ch 1) 4 times in next ch-3 sp, sc in next ch-3 sp, ch 1] around, join in 3rd ch of beg ch-4. Fasten off.

Rnd 4: With size 10 hook, join delft in first dc of previous rnd, *[ch 2, sk next ch-1 sp, sl st in next dc] 3 times, (dc, ch 2, dc) in next sc**, sl st in next dc, rep from * around, ending last rep at **, sl st in same st as beg sl st. Fasten off.

Fold cuff down.

Sock Trim No. 2
Make 2.
Rnd 1: Unroll cuff of sock; working on WS of sock with size 9 hook and frosty green, place slip knot on hook, push hook through top edge of sock, yo, draw through sock, yo draw through 2 lps on hook, work 39 [43, 47]

sc around top edge, **join** *(see Pattern Notes)* in first sc. Fasten off. *(40 [44, 48] sc)*

Rnd 2: With size 10 hook, working in **front lps** *(see Stitch Guide)*, join white in first sc, ch 1, sc in same sc as beg ch-1, ch 3, sk next sc, [sc in next sc, ch 3, sk next sc] around, join in first sc. *(20 [22, 24] ch-3 sps)*

Rnd 3: Sl st in next ch-3 sp, (ch 3, dc, ch 2, 2 dc) in same ch sp, sc in next ch-3 sp, [(2 dc, ch 2, 2 dc) in next ch-3 sp, sc in next ch-3 sp] around, join in 3rd ch of beg ch-3. Fasten off.

Rnd 4: With size 10 hook, join frosty green in any ch-2 sp, ch 1, (sc, ch 3, sc) in same ch-2 sp, sk next dc, *sc dec *(see Stitch Guide)* in next 2 dc, sk next dc**, (sc, ch 3, sc) in next ch-2 sp, sk next dc, rep from * around, ending last rep at **, join in beg sc. Fasten off. ●

Sweetie Pie Baby

Design by Kathleen Stuart

Skill Level
■■□□ EASY

Finished Size
11 inches tall

Materials
- Sport weight yarn:
    2 oz pink, 1 oz off-white, scrap of each pale yellow, red and light brown
- Size G/6/4mm crochet hook or size needed to obtain gauge
- Stitch marker
- Fiberfill
- Tapestry needle

Gauge
5 sc = 1 inch

Pattern Notes
Weave in loose ends as work progresses.
Do not join rnds unless otherwise stated; use a stitch marker to mark rounds.

Head & Body
Rnd 1: Starting at top of head, with off-white, ch 2, 6 sc in 2nd ch from hook. *(6 sc)*

Rnd 2: 2 sc in each sc around. *(12 sc)*

Rnd 3: [Sc in next sc, 2 sc in next sc] rep around. *(18 sc)*

Rnd 4: [Sc in each of next 2 sc, 2 sc in next sc] rep around. *(24 sc)*

Rnd 5: [Sc in each of next 3 sc, 2 sc in next sc] rep around. *(30 sc)*

Rnd 6: [Sc in each of next 4 sc, 2 sc in next sc] rep around. *(36 sc)*

Rnds 7–12: Sc in each sc around.

Rnd 13: [Sc in each of next 4 sc, sc dec over next 2 sc] rep around. *(30 sc)*

Rnd 14: [Sc in each of next 3 sc, sc dec over next 2 sc] rep around. *(24 sc)*

Rnd 15: [Sc in each of next 2 sc, sc dec over next 2 sc] rep around. *(18 sc)*

Stuff Head with fiberfill.

Rnd 16: [Sc in next st, sc dec over next 2 sc] rep around, changing to pink in last sc. *(12 sc)*

Rnds 17 & 18: Working with pink, rep rnds 3 and 4. *(24 sc)*

Rnd 19: [Dc in each of next 3 sc, 2 dc in next sc] rep around. *(30 dc)*

Rnd 20: [Dc in each of next 4 dc, 2 dc in next dc] rep around. *(36 dc)*

Rnds 21–29: Dc in each dc around.

Stuff Body with fiberfill.

First Leg
Rnd 1: Dc in each of next 9 dc, sk next 18 dc, dc in each of next 9 dc. *(18 dc)*

Rnds 2–8: Dc in each dc around.

Rnd 9: [Dc in next dc, dc dec over next 2 sts] rep around. *(12 dc)*

Rnd 10: [Dc dec over next 2 dc] 6 times, sl st in next st, leaving a length of yarn, fasten off.

Stuff Leg with fiberfill and sew leg opening closed.

2nd Leg

Rnd 1: Attach pink in next unworked st of rnd 29 of body, ch 3 (counts as first dc), dc in each of next 17 dc. *(18 dc)*

Rnds 2–10: Rep rnds 2–10 of first leg.

With a length of pink, sew crotch opening closed.

Arm

Make 2

Rnd 1: With pink, ch 2, 6 sc in 2nd ch from hook.

Rnd 2: 2 dc in each sc around. *(12 dc)*

Rnds 3–9: Dc in each dc around, changing to off-white in last st of rnd 9.

Stuff Arm with fiberfill as work progresses.

Rnds 10 & 11: Dc in each dc around.

Rnd 12: [Dc dec over next 2 dc] rep around, sl st in next st, leaving a length of yarn, fasten off.

Sew Arm to side of Body over rnds 17–19.

Bonnet

Rnds 1–6: With pink, rep rnds 1–6 of Head & Body. *(36 sc)*

Rnd 7: [Sc in each of next 5 sc, 2 sc in next sc] rep around. *(42 sc)*

Rnd 8: [Sc in each of next 6 sc, 2 sc in next sc] rep around. *(48 sc)*

Rnd 9: [Sc in each of next 7 sc, 2 sc in next sc] rep around. *(54 sc)*

Rnd 10: [Sc in each of next 8 sc, 2 sc in next sc] rep around. *(60 sc)*

Row 11: Now working in rows, in back lps only, work 2 dc in each of next 49 sts, [dc, ch 3, sl st] in next st, leaving rem 10 sts unworked, fasten off.

Finishing

Using photo as a guide, work eyes over rnd 8 of Head, leaving 2 sc free between eyes; with light brown, embroider V-shape for each eye.

With red, embroider smiley mouth centered below eyes over rnds 11 and 12 of Head.

For hair, wrap pale yellow around 2 fingers several times, remove lps from fingers and sew at center front of head over rnd 2.

Weave a 10-inch length of pink yarn through base of dc sts of row 11, leaving beg and ending lengths equal; place bonnet on head, pull ends gently and double-knot under chin, tie ends in a bow and trim ends even. Thread tapestry needle with a length of pink and sew bonnet to head. ●

Nursery Choo Choo

Designs by Donna Collinsworth

Skill Level

■■□□ EASY

Finished Sizes
Engine: 7 x 8 inches
Freight car: 4½ x 6 inches

Materials
- Medium (worsted) weight yarn:
  2 oz (140 yds, 60g) each
  3 scrap colors
- Size H/8/5mm crochet hook
  or size needed to obtain gauge
- 1½-inch-diameter wooden wheels: 12
- 36-inch-long, ¼-inch-diameter
  wooden dowel
- Yarn needle
- Polyester fiberfill
- Hook-and-loop closure
- Coordinating colors of felt
- Craft glue

Gauge
4 sts = 1 inch

Train Engine
Base
Long Side
Make 2.
Ch 21.

Row 1: Sc in 2nd ch from hook, [dc in next ch, sc in next ch] 9 times; dc in last ch, turn. *(20 sts)*

Row 2: Ch 1, sc in first dc, dc in next sc, [sc in next dc, dc in next sc] 9 times, turn.

Row 3: Ch 1, sc in first dc, dc in next sc, [sc in next dc, dc in next sc] 9 times.

Fasten off and weave in ends.

Short Side
Make 2.
Ch 15.

Row 1: Sc in 2nd ch from hook, [dc in next ch, sc in next ch] 6 times; dc in last ch, turn. *(14 sts)*

Row 2: Ch 1, sc in first dc, dc in next sc, [sc in next st, dc in next st] 6 times, turn.

Row 3: Ch 1, sc in first dc, dc in next sc, [sc in next dc, dc in next sc] 6 times.

Fasten off and weave in ends.

Top/Bottom
Make 2.
Ch 21.

Row 1: Sc in 2nd ch from hook, [dc in next ch, sc in next ch] 9 times; dc in last ch, turn. *(20 sts)*

Row 2: Ch 1, sc in first dc, dc in next sc, [sc in next dc, dc in next sc] 9 times, turn.

Rows 3–10: Rep row 2. At end of row 10, fasten off and weave in ends.

Connector
Ch 5.

Row 1: Sc in 2nd ch from hook, dc in next ch, sc in next ch, dc in last ch, turn. *(4 sts)*

Row 2: Ch 1, sc in first dc, dc in next sc, sc in next dc, dc in next sc, turn.

Rows 3 & 4: Rep row 2. At end of row 4, fasten off and weave in ends.

Axle Pocket
Make 2.
Ch 13.

Row 1: Sc in 2nd ch from hook, [dc in next ch, sc in next ch] 5 times; dc in last ch, turn. *(12 sts)*

Row 2: Ch 1, sc in first dc, dc in next sc [sc in next dc, dc in next sc] 5 times, turn.

Row 3: Ch 1, sc in first dc, dc in next sc, [sc in next dc, dc in next sc] 5 times.

Fasten off and weave in ends.

Base Assembly
With tapestry needle and matching yarn, sew each Long Side to 1 Short Side. Sew rem Short Side to Long Sides forming rectangle. Sew Bottom to rectangle. Sew Top across 3 Sides. Stuff with fiberfill and sew opening closed. Measure ¼ inch from each end of Bottom of Base and sew Axle Pockets to Bottom. Cut 2 (5-inch) lengths of dowel. Slide through Axle Pockets. Glue wheels to ends of dowels, being sure dowels extend to outer edge of wheel.

Stuff Connector and sew to center of 1 short end of Base. Sew small square of lp part of hook-and-loop closure to center of end of Connector.

Cab
Long Side
Make 2.
Ch 15.

Row 1: Sc in 2nd ch from hook, [dc in next ch, sc in next ch] 6 times; dc in last ch, turn. *(14 sts)*

Row 2: Ch 1, sc in first dc, dc in next sc, [sc in next dc, dc in next sc] 6 times, turn.

Rows 3–13: Rep row 2. At end of row 13, fasten off and weave in ends.

Top & Short Sides
Make 3.
Ch 9.

Row 1: Sc in 2nd ch from hook, [dc in next ch, sc in next ch] 3 times; dc in last ch, turn. *(8 sts)*

Row 2: Ch 1, sc in next dc, dc in next sc, [sc in next dc, dc in next sc] 3 times, turn.

Rows 3–13: Rep row 2. At end of row 13, fasten off and weave in ends.

Cab Assembly
With tapestry needle and matching yarn, sew Long and Short Sides tog to form tall rectangle; sew Top to rectangle. Stuff with fiberfill. Referring to photo for placement, sew to top of Base, keeping back of Cab even with back of Base (end with Connector attached). Cut 2 (1½ x 2-inch) pieces of felt and 1 (4 x 1½-inch) piece of felt for Cab windows. Referring to photo for placement, glue to Cab.

Engine
Ch 4, join to form a ring.

Rnd 1: Ch 1, 12 sc in ring; join in first sc, turn. *(12 sc)*

Rnd 2: Ch 1, sc in first sc, dc in next sc, [sc in next sc, dc in next sc] 5 times; join in first sc, turn.

Rnds 3–14: Rep rnd 2. At end of rnd 14, fasten off and weave in ends.

Engine Assembly

Stuff with fiberfill and sew to front of cab. Cut 1 (1-inch-diameter) circle and 1 (⅝-inch-diameter) circle from felt. Glue smaller circle to center of large circle; glue large circle to front of Engine.

Smokestack

Ch 4, join to form a ring.

Rnd 1: Ch 1, 8 sc in ring; join in first sc, turn. *(8 sc)*

Rnd 2: In each sc work (sc, dc); join in first sc, turn. *(16 sts)*

Rnd 3: Ch 1, sc in first dc, dc in next sc, [sc in next dc, dc in next sc] 7 times; join in first sc, turn.

Rnd 4: Rep rnd 3.

Note: *For dc dec, [yo, draw up lp in st indicated, yo, draw through 2 lps on hook] twice; yo and draw through all 3 lps on hook.*

Rnd 5: Ch 1, sc in first dc, **dc dec** *(see Note)* over next 2 sts, sk next st, *sc in next st, dc in next st; rep from * across; join in first sc, turn. *(14 sts)*

Rnds 6 & 7: Rep rnd 5.

Rnd 8: Ch 1, sc in first dc, dc dec over next 2 sts, sk next st, *sc in next st, dc in next st; rep from * across; join in first sc, turn. *(8 sts)*

Rnd 9: Ch 1, sc in first dc, dc in next sc, [sc in next st, dc in next st] 3 times; join in first sc, turn.

Rnds 10–12: Rep rnd 9. At end of rnd 12, fasten off and weave in ends.

Smokestack Assembly

Stuff Smokestack with fiberfill. Referring to photo for placement, sew to Engine.

Cow Catcher

Side

Make 2.

Ch 3.

Row 1: Sc in 2nd ch from hook, dc in next ch, turn. *(2 sts)*

Row 2: Ch 1, in each st work (sc, dc), turn. *(4 sts)*

Row 3: Ch 1, sc in first dc, dc in next sc, sc in next dc, dc in next sc, turn.

Rows 4 & 5: Rep row 3.

Row 6: Ch 1, in each of first 2 sts work (sc, dc); sc in next dc, dc in next sc, turn. *(6 sts)*

Row 7: Ch 1, sc in first dc, dc in next sc, [sc in next dc, dc in next sc] twice.

Fasten off and weave in ends.

Top/Bottom

Make 2.

Ch 3.

Row 1: Sc in 2nd ch from hook, dc in next ch, turn. *(2 sts)*

Row 2: Ch 1, in each st work (sc, dc), turn. *(4 sts)*

Row 3: Ch 1, in each st work (sc, dc), turn. *(8 sts)*

Row 4: Ch 1, sc in first dc, dc in next sc, [sc in next st, dc in next st] 3 times, turn.

Row 5: In each of first 2 sts work (sc, dc); [sc in next st, dc in next st] twice; in each of next 2 sts work (sc, dc). *(12 sts)*

Fasten off and weave in ends.

Cow Catcher Assembly

With tapestry needle and matching yarn, sew 2 long edges of Sides tog. Sew 1 Top and 1 Bottom to Side to make a triangle. Stuff with fiberfill and sew to front of Base of Engine. Cut 6 (¼ x 2½-inch) pieces of felt. Referring to photo for placement, glue to Cow Catcher, trimming ends if necessary to fit.

Freight Car

Make 2.

Base

Long Side

Make 2.

Ch 21.

Row 1: Sc in 2nd ch from hook, [dc in next ch, sc in next ch] 9 times; dc in last ch, turn. *(20 sts)*

Row 2: Ch 1, sc in first dc, dc in next sc [sc in next dc, dc in next sc] 9 times, turn.

Rows 3–5: Rep row 2. At end of row 5, fasten off and weave in ends.

Short Side

Make 2.

Ch 15.

Row 1: Sc in 2nd ch from hook, [dc in next ch, sc in next ch] 6 times; dc in last ch, turn. *(14 sts)*

Row 2: Ch 1, sc in first dc, dc in next sc, [sc in next st, dc in next st] 6 times, turn.

Rows 3–5: Rep row 2. At end of row 5, fasten off and weave in ends.

Top/Bottom

Make 2.

Work same as Top/Bottom for Train Engine.

Connector

Work same as Connector for Train Engine.

Axle Pocket

Make 2.

Work same as Axle Pocket for Train Engine.

Assembly

Sew Long and Short Sides tog to form rectangle. Sew rectangle to top of Base. Sew Connector to 1 end (back) of 1 Freight Car. Sew small square of lp part of hook-and-loop closure to end of Connector and hook part of hook-and-loop closure to opposite end (front) of Base. Sew small square of hook part of hook-and-loop closure to 1 end (front) of rem Freight Car. •

Twinkle Blanket

Design by Aline Suplinskas

Skill Level

■□□□ BEGINNER

Finished Size

26 x 32 inches

Materials

- Caron Cuddlesoft Pomp fine (sport) weight yarn (1¾ oz per skein): 2 skeins each #2814 baby blue, #2830 rainbow print and #2811 baby green
- Size H/8/5mm crochet hook or size needed to obtain gauge
- Yarn needle

Gauge

[Sc, ch 2, dc] twice = 1½ inches; 3 rows = 1 inch

Pattern Notes

Weave in loose ends as work progresses.

Do not fasten off yarns at end of rows, drop old color and complete last step of last sc with new color.

Blanket

Row 1: With baby blue, ch 155, dc in 3rd ch from hook, sk each of next 3 chs, [{sc, ch 2, dc} in next ch, sk each of next 3 chs] 37 times, sc in last ch, changing to rainbow print in last step of sc, turn.

Row 2: Ch 3, dc in same st as beg ch-3, [{sc, ch 2, dc} in next ch-2 sp] rep across, ending with sc in last ch sp, changing to baby green in last step of sc, turn.

Row 3: Rep row 2, changing to baby blue in last step of sc, turn.

Row 4: Rep row 2, changing to rainbow print in last step of sc, turn.

Rows 5–92: Rep row 2, maintaining the established color sequence.

At the end of row 92, fasten off baby blue and rainbow print yarns, leaving baby green, turn.

Trim

Rnd 1: Ch 1, [sc, ch 2, dc] twice in end st for corner, working down side edge of rows, sk next row, [{sc, ch 2, dc} in side edge of next row, sk next row] rep to bottom corner, [sc, ch 2, dc] twice in first ch of opposite side of foundation ch, [sk next 3 chs, {sc, ch 2, dc} in next ch] rep across to last 4 chs, sk next ch, [sc, ch 2, dc] twice in end ch, working across side edge of rows, sk next row, [{sc, ch 2, dc} in side of next row, sk next row] rep across to first st of last row of blanket, [sc, ch 2, dc] twice in end st for corner, [sc, ch 2, dc] in each ch-2 sp across, fasten off. ●

Pacifier Holders

Finders Keepers
Design by Sharon Ballsmith

Skill Level
◀■■■□ INTERMEDIATE

Finished Size
9 inches long, excluding clip

Materials
- Size 10 crochet cotton:
  22 yds yellow
- Size 1/2.25mm steel crochet hook
  or size needed to obtain gauge
- Tapestry needle
- Dritz® suspender/mitten 1-inch clips
  (enough for 2 Pacifier Keepers)
- Pacifier with handle

Gauge
8 hdc = 1 inch; rows 3–9 of Strap = 1 inch

Pattern Notes
Weave in loose ends as work progresses.

Join with slip stitch as indicated unless otherwise stated.

Row 3 only, chain-2 at beginning of row counts as first half double crochet.

Rows 4–50, chain-2 at beginning of rows, does not count as first half double crochet, but brings yarn to level of working row.

Pacifier Keeper
Pacifier Loop
Row 1: Ch 26, sc in **back bar** *(see illustration)* of 2nd ch from hook, sc in back bar of each ch across. *(25 sc)*

Row 2: To close Pacifier Loop, work to crochet along side in end of row, ch 1, 2 sc evenly sp across end, now bring up opposite end *(as in u-shape, using care not to twist)*, work 2 sc evenly sp across end, turn. *(4 sc)*

Strap
Row 3: Ch 2 *(see Pattern Notes)*, hdc in first sc, [2 hdc in each sc] across, turn. *(8 hdc)*

Row 4: Ch 2, 2 hdc in sp between first 2 sts, [sk next 2 sts, 2 hdc in next sp] 3 times, turn. *(8 hdc)*

Row 5: Ch 2, sk first 2 hdc, 2 hdc in next sp between sts, [sk next 2 sts, 2 hdc in sp between sts] 3 times, turn. *(8 hdc)*

Rows 6–50: Rep row 5.

Row 51: Ch 1, 2 sc in first hdc, sc in each of next 6 hdc, 2 sc in last hdc, sk last ch-2 sp, turn. *(10 sc)*

Rows 52–57: Ch 1, sc in each sc across, turn. At the end of last rep, leaving 12-inch length, fasten off.

Finishing
Fold end of Strap over bar of clip and sew row 57 to row 52. Pull lp end of Pacifier Keeper through handle of pacifier, pull clip end through lp end and pull to tighten. Fasten clip end to baby's clothing.

Back Bar of Ch

Dragonfly Holder

Design by Darla Sims

Skill Level

◼◼◼◻ INTERMEDIATE

Finished Size

4½ inches wide x 5¾ inches long,
excluding pacifier

Materials

- TLC Cotton Plus medium (worsted) weight
  yarn (3½ oz/178 yds/100g per skein):
  - 10 yds each #3643 kiwi
    and #3590 lavender
  - 3 yds each #3811 medium blue
    and #3222 yellow
- Size E/4/3.5mm crochet hook
  or size needed to obtain gauge
- Tapestry needle
- Sewing needle and thread
- Pacifier

Gauge

Small Wing = 1½ inches in diameter;
Large Wing = 2¼ inches in diameter

Pattern Notes

Weave in loose ends as work progresses.

Join with slip stitch as indicated unless
otherwise stated.

Dragonfly

Tail

Row 1 (RS): With kiwi, ch 19, sl st in 2nd ch from hook, sl st in each rem ch across to last ch.

Body

Row 1 (RS): Ch 1, 5 sc in last ch, turn. *(5 sc)*

Rows 2–7: Ch 1, sc in each sc across, turn.

Row 8: Sl st in first 2 sc, 5 sc in 3rd sc, draw up lp, remove hook, insert hook in first sc of 5-sc group, pick up dropped lp and draw through st on hook, sl st in last 2 sc of row 7. Leaving 12-inch length of yarn, fasten off.

Thread rem length on tapestry needle, sew ends of rows 2–7 tog to form Body in a tube.

Thread 4-inch length of kiwi yarn through center front of head and tie ends in a knot. Trim ends to measure approximately 1 inch.

Small Wing

Make 2.

Rnd 1: With medium blue, ch 2, 5 sc in 2nd ch from hook, **join** *(see Pattern Notes)* in first sc. Fasten off. *(5 sc)*

Rnd 2: Join yellow with sc in any st, sc in same st, 2 sc in each rem sc around, join in first sc. Fasten off. *(10 sc)*

Rnd 3: Join lavender with sc in any st, sc in same st, 2 sc in each rem sc around, join in first sc. Fasten off. *(20 sc)*

Large Wing

Make 2.

Rnd 1: With medium blue, ch 2, 5 sc in 2nd ch from hook, join in first sc. Fasten off. *(5 sc)*

Rnd 2: Join yellow with sc in any st, sc in same st, 2 sc in each rem sc around, join in first sc. Fasten off. *(10 sc)*

Rnd 3: Join lavender with sc in any st, sc in same st, 2 sc in each rem sc around, join in first sc. *(20 sc)*

Rnd 4: Sl st in each of next 3 sc, sc in each of next 3 sc, 2 hdc in each of next 8 sc, sc in each of next 3 sc, sl st in next 3 sc. Fasten off. *(28 sts)*

Finishing

Thread 12-inch length of lavender on tapestry needle. With RS of Small Wings facing, working through both thicknesses, sew across 3 sts of rnd 3 and sew to underside lower portion of Body.

With RS of Large Wings facing and hdc sts at top and outer edge, working through both thicknesses, sew tog the 3 sc sts worked before the hdc sts. Position the Large Wings on underside of body with hdc sts at top outer edge and sl sts under Small Wings, sew center to Body and lower portion of Large Wings to Small Wings.

With sewing needle and thread, fold end of Tail over pacifier handle and sew in place. •

Standard Yarn Weight System

Categories of yarn, gauge ranges, and recommended needle and hook sizes

Yarn Weight Symbol & Category Names	1 SUPER FINE	2 FINE	3 LIGHT	4 MEDIUM	5 BULKY	6 SUPER BULKY
Type of Yarns in Category	Sock, Fingering, Baby	Sport, Baby	DK, Light Worsted	Worsted, Afghan, Aran	Chunky, Craft, Rug	Super Chunky, Roving
Crochet Gauge* Ranges in Single Crochet to 4 inches	21–32 sts	16–20 sts	12–17 sts	11–14 sts	8–11 sts	5–9 sts
Recommended Hook in Metric Size Range	2.25–3.5mm	3.5–4.5mm	4.5–4.5mm	5.5–6.5mm	6.5–9mm	9mm and larger
Recommended Hook U.S. Size Range	B1–E4	E4-7	7–I-9	I-9–K-10½	K-10½–M-13	M-13 and larger

* **GUIDELINES ONLY:** The above reflect the most commonly used gauges and hook sizes for specific yarn categories.

Skill Levels

BEGINNER

Projects for first-time crocheters using basic stitches and minimal shaping.

EASY

Easy projects using basic stitches, repetitive stitch patterns, simple color changes and simple shaping and finishing.

INTERMEDIATE

Intermediate projects with a variety of stitches, mid-level shaping and finishing.

EXPERIENCED

Experienced projects using advanced techniques and stitches, detailed shaping and refined finishing.

Symbols

* **An asterisk** is used to mark the beginning of a portion of instructions to be worked more than once; thus, "rep from * twice more" means after working the instructions once, repeat the instructions following the asterisk twice more (3 times in all).

( ) **Parentheses** are used to set off and clarify a group of stitches that are to be worked all into the same space or stitch, such as "in next corner sp work (2 dc, ch 1, 2 dc)."

[ ] **Brackets** are used to enclose instructions that should be worked the exact number of times specified immediately following the brackets, such as "[2 sc in next dc, sc in next dc] twice."

[ ] Brackets and ( ) parentheses are used to provide additional information to clarify instructions.

STITCH GUIDE

FOR MORE COMPLETE INFORMATION, VISIT **FREEPATTERNS.COM**

STITCH ABBREVIATIONS

beg .... begin/begins/beginning
bpdc .... back post double crochet
bpsc .... back post single crochet
bptr .... back post treble crochet
CC .... contrasting color
ch(s) ....chain(s)
ch- .... refers to chain or space
previously made (i.e., ch-1 space)
ch sp(s) .... chain space(s)
cl(s) .... cluster(s)
cm .... centimeter(s)
dc .... double crochet (singular/plural)
dc dec .... double crochet 2 or more
stitches together, as indicated
dec .... decrease/decreases/decreasing
dtr .... double treble crochet
ext ....extended
fpdc .... front post double crochet
fpsc .... front post single crochet
fptr .... front post treble crochet
g ....gram(s)
hdc .... half double crochet
hdc dec .... half double crochet 2 or more
stitches together, as indicated
inc .... increase/increases/increasing
lp(s) ....loop(s)
MC ....main color
mm .... millimeter(s)
oz ....ounce(s)
pc .... popcorn(s)
rem .... remain/remains/remaining
rep(s) ....repeat(s)
rnd(s) ....round(s)
RS ....right side
sc .... single crochet (singular/plural)
sc dec ....single crochet 2 or more
stitches together, as indicated
sk ....skip/skipped/skipping
sl st(s) .... slip stitch(es)
sp(s) .... space(s)/spaced
st(s) ....stitch(es)
tog ....together
tr.. treble crochet
trtr...triple treble
WS .... wrong side
yd(s) ....yard(s)
yo ....yarn over

YARN CONVERSION

OUNCES TO GRAMS		GRAMS TO OUNCES	
1	28.4	25	7/8
2	56.7	40	1 2/3
3	85.0	50	1 3/4
4	113.4	100	3 1/2

UNITED STATES		UNITED KINGDOM
sl st (slip stitch)	=	sc (single crochet)
sc (single crochet)	=	dc (double crochet)
hdc (half double crochet)	=	htr (half treble crochet)
dc (double crochet)	=	tr (treble crochet)
tr (treble crochet)	=	dtr (double treble crochet)
dtr (double treble crochet)	=	ttr (triple treble crochet)
skip	=	miss

Reverse Single Crochet (reverse sc): Ch 1. Skip first st. [Working from left to right, insert hook in next st from front to back, draw up lp on hook, yo, and draw through both lps on hook.]

Chain (ch): Yo, pull through lp on hook.

Single crochet (sc): Insert hook in st, yo, pull through st, yo, pull through both lps on hook.

Double crochet (dc): Yo, insert hook in st, yo, pull through st, [yo, pull through 2 lps] twice.

Front loop (front lp) Back loop (back lp)
Front Loop   Back Loop

Front post stitch (fp): Back post stitch (bp): When working post st, insert hook from right to left around post st on previous row.
Back   Front
Post of Stitch

Half double crochet (hdc): Yo, insert hook in st, yo, pull through st, yo, pull through all 3 lps on hook.

Double treble crochet (dtr): Yo 3 times, insert hook in st, yo, pull through st, [yo, pull through 2 lps] 4 times.

Slip stitch (sl st): Insert hook in st, pull through both lps on hook.

Chain Color Change (ch color change) Yo with new color, draw through last lp on hook.

Double Crochet Color Change (dc color change) Drop first color, yo with new color, draw through last 2 lps of st.

Treble crochet (tr): Yo twice, insert hook in st, yo, pull through st, [yo, pull through 2 lps] 3 times.

Single crochet decrease (sc dec): (Insert hook, yo, draw lp through) in each of the sts indicated, yo, draw through all lps on hook.

Example of 2-sc dec

Half double crochet decrease (hdc dec): (Yo, insert hook, yo, draw lp through) in each of the sts indicated, yo, draw through all lps on hook.

Example of 2-hdc dec

Double crochet decrease (dc dec): Yo, insert hook, yo, draw loop through, draw through 2 lps on hook) in each of the sts indicated, yo, draw through all lps on hook.

Example of 2-dc dec

Treble crochet decrease (tr dec): Holding back last lp of each st, tr in each of the sts indicated, yo, pull through all lps on hook.

Example of 2-tr dec

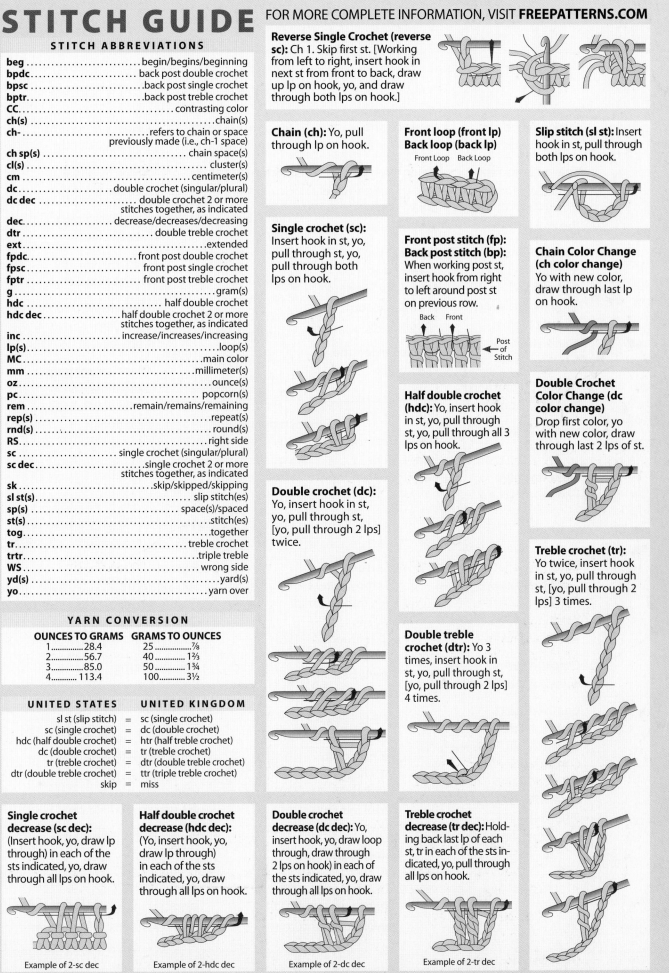

Special Thanks

Mickie Akins
Baby Squares

Sharon Ballsmith
Finders Keepers,
Merry Go 'Round
the Block

Sue Childress
Bonnet & Booties,
Embellished
Slippers, Little Man
Christening Set,
Shells Stitch Papoose
& Hat

Donna Collinsworth
Nursery Choo Choo

Norma Gale
Sock Trims

Ellen Gormley
Fisherman's Hat

Paula Gron
Baby Biker Bibs

Helen Heaverin
Duck Hooded Towel
& Bath Mitt, Pig
Security Blanket

Frances Hughes
Baby Headbands,
Mary Jane Slippers,
Shell & Popcorn
Papoose Set

Lucille LaFlamme
Overall Bib

Lisa Naskrent
Pretty Edgings

Nancy Nehring
Baby Cloche,
Baby Hat

Joyce Nordstrom
Hooded Baby Gown

Shirley Patterson
Flower Garden Ball

Diane Simpson
Frilly Dress,
Short Top Socks

Darla Sims
Baby Delight,
Dragonfly Holder,
Nursing Pillow

Mary Ann Sipes
Rosebuds,
Tiny Balloons

Dianne Stein
Boy's Striped Hat &
Sweater, Girl's Striped
Hat & Sweater

Lindsey Stephens
Bon Appétit Bib

Arline Suplinskas
Twinkle Blanket

Kathleen Stuart
Sweetie Pie Baby

Dorothy Warrell
Little Lamb Set

Michele Wilcox
Bear Diaper Cover &
Cap, Toy Cat, Toy Dog

Glenda Winkleman
Baby Blocks Afghan
& Pillow Set, Baby's
First Book

Buyer's Guide

Caron International
Customer Service
P.O. Box 222
Washington, NC 27889
www.caron.com

Cascade Yarns
www.cascadeyarns.com

Coats & Clark
Creme de la Creme, J. & P.
Coats Royale, Red Heart, TLC
Consumer Services
P.O. Box 12229
Greenville, SC 29612-0229
(800) 648-1479
www.coatsandclark.com

Berroco Inc.
Wendy/Peter Pan
14 Elmdale Road
P.O. Box 367
Uxbridge, MA 01569
(508) 278-2527
www.berroco.com
www.tbramsden.co.uk

K.F.I.
Katia
P.O. Box 336
315 Bayview Ave.
Amityville, NY 11701
(516) 546-3600
www.knittingfever.com

Lion Brand Yarn
135 Kero Road
Carlstadt, NJ 07072
(800) 258-YARN (9276)
www.lionbrand.com

Plymouth Yarn Co.
500 Lafayette St.
Bristol, PA 19007
(215) 788-0459
www.plymouthyarn.com

Spinrite Yarns
Bernat, Lily
320 Livingstone Ave. S.
Listowel, ON
N4W 3H3 Canada
(888) 368-8401
www.spinriteyarns.com
www.bernat.com
www.sugarncream.com

Westminster Fibers Inc.
Schachenmayer
165 Ledge St.
Nashua, NH 03060
(800) 445-9276
www.westminsterfibers.com